"*Just a Thought* helps you see why you suffer, and it shows you how to wake up to your innate well-being."

—**Deepak Chopra, MD**, author of *Total Meditation*

"*Just a Thought* is a must-read for anyone who feels broken or inadequate. Amy offers a radical approach to discovering peace of mind that is much simpler than conventional self-help. Follow her guidance, and you will discover the happiness, confidence, and well-being you never thought were possible. This book has the power to change your life!"

—**Gail Brenner, PhD**, author of *The End of Self-Help* and *Suffering Is Optional*

"*Just a Thought* provides a road map to freedom of mind across a range of seemingly insurmountable issues. Discovering the way our mind works and learning how to react to it is a game changer for escaping anxiety, fear, and unnecessary harsh self-judgments. The book delivers on all fronts—a gentle, reassuring journey of discovering *who we are* by understanding *what we're not*. True freedom from repetitive negative behaviors."

—**John C. Dicey**, global CEO, senior therapist, and coauthor at Allen Carr's Easyway Worldwide

"This beautifully written and powerful book untangles so much of the confusion we feel every day, providing a simple and elegant alternative to the maddening cycles of the mind. This book distills some of the most complex concepts into usable, practical direction to find peace beyond your thoughts. A truly incredible, and life-changing read."

—**Annie Grace**, author of *This Naked Mind*

JUST *a* THOUGHT

**A No-Willpower Approach *to*
Overcome Self-Doubt &
Make Peace *with* Your Mind**

AMY JOHNSON, PHD

New Harbinger Publications, Inc.

Publisher's Note

This publication is designed to provide accurate and authoritative information in regard to the subject matter covered. It is sold with the understanding that the publisher is not engaged in rendering psychological, financial, legal, or other professional services. If expert assistance or counseling is needed, the services of a competent professional should be sought.

Distributed in Canada by Raincoast Books

NEW HARBINGER PUBLICATIONS is a registered trademark of New Harbinger Publications, Inc.

Cover design by Sara Christian; Acquired by Elizabeth Hollis Hansen; Edited by Gretel Hakanson

Library of Congress Cataloging-in-Publication Data

Names: Johnson, Amy (Psychologist)
Title: Just a thought / Amy Johnson.
Description: Oakland, CA : New Harbinger Publications, Inc., [2021] | Includes bibliographical references.
Identifiers: LCCN 2021019761 | ISBN 9781684038183 (trade paperback)
Subjects: LCSH: Negativism. | Habit breaking. | Behavior modification.
Classification: LCC BF698.35.N44 J64 2021 | DDC 158.1--dc23
LC record available at https://lccn.loc.gov/2021019761

Printed in the United States of America

23   22   21

10   9   8   7   6   5   4   3   2

To The Little School of Big Change community. You have taught me so much. It's an honor to watch you discover more of who you are every day.

CONTENTS

PREFACE

I have been listening to people tell me about their struggles, fears, insecurities, insights, hopes, and wishes for as long as I can remember. First, as the friend whom everyone loved to confide in. Later, as the neighborhood bartender. Following that, as a social psychologist. And, for the past fifteen years, as a professional coach and teacher.

I've had thousands of private coaching conversations, run hundreds of group coaching sessions, and lead an online school and community where I hear from people from all over the world every day.

A funny thing happens when you hear the innermost thoughts and feelings of that many people, that often, over that many years.

You see that we're all the same.

Demographics, childhood, and life experiences don't make us fundamentally different. Those might impact *what* we talk about, but they don't impact the fact that our mind talks, just like everyone else's. Beyond the surface layer of always-shifting story and opinion, we all work in the same way.

Our minds spit out repetitive stories. They love to replay the past and predict the future.

Our minds have strong opinions that feel solid and meaningful, but are always changing and contradicting themselves.

Our minds love drama and exaggeration. They relate everything back to the person they inhabit—our mind's world revolves around us.

Minds love certainty and efficiency. They create our identities and then work like crazy to protect their creation.

When we see how our mind works, it becomes easier to not take it so personally or seriously. Its habitual stories, complaints, fears, and criticisms move to the background. Our awareness shifts from the *content* of our moment-to-moment experience to something quieter and deeper that lies *beyond* our moment-to-moment experience.

We live less in the stories and details of *what* our mind is saying and more in the recognition *that* a mind is talking. And a whole new world—beyond the habitual hum of thought—opens up.

Years of day in and day out listening has shown me that, without exception, we're all the same. Only the details are different, and the details aren't nearly as relevant or meaningful as we think they are.

It's shown me that, without exception, we are all fundamentally well. When we think our mind's stories mean something solid about who we are, we suffer. When we see the truth—and we

glimpse the space that lies beyond those thought-created stories—
we suffer far less.

One of the phrases I find myself saying most often is: "That's just what minds do."

Minds compare and worry and project and judge. They label and categorize and fear and complain. All eight billion of them. Different details, same process.

When we see that the machine in our head is just doing what the machine in a head does, everything changes. Habits and anxiety begin to fall away. Insecurities and self-judgments look less real. Problems and limitations appear far less solid.

As we wake up to the psychological, repetitive nature of the mind, we also get to wake up to who and what is there beyond it.

We get to know who we are by knowing what we're not.

INTRODUCTION

There are these two young fish swimming along, and they happen to meet an older fish swimming the other way, who nods at them and says, "Morning, boys. How's the water?" And the two young fish swim on for a bit, and then eventually one of them looks over at the other and goes, "What the hell is water?" —David Foster Wallace

LUCY, ASLEEP

Lucy kept her world small.

She was in her early forties and had been an administrative assistant for an accounting firm for nine years. She was good at her job and friendly enough with her coworkers. But nearly every morning as she walked from the shaded spot where she parked her unassuming hatchback past the downstairs doorman, weaving through dozens of busy people also beginning their day to her tidy desk in her firm's sixth-floor office, her mind repeated its routine plan of action.

Lucy told me her biggest fear was making a mistake, but if you asked her to elaborate on that, she couldn't. It didn't make sense. She was an accounting admin, not a brain surgeon. She scheduled appointments and kept an office running—not always easy work, but not life or death.

When I asked Lucy what she imagined happening, I watched her mind hunt for something logical to grab on to. She didn't know, really; she just felt a compulsion to hide. She said she was afraid of disappointing others, afraid of what they would think, but her fears were vague and slippery.

Even though Lucy couldn't nail down what she was afraid of, the *feeling* of fear was anything but vague. The feeling was visceral and emotional. Because it felt so strong and all-consuming, Lucy assumed the fear must be warning her of a real threat. It must be holding her back, keeping her tethered to her mind-made comfort zone out of necessity, she reasoned. Why else would she feel this fear so regularly?

Because Lucy couldn't see through her limitations, she assumed they were valid and true. But the real reason she couldn't see through them is because the limitations themselves were made of thought. Her mind created these fuzzy fears and worries, and that same mind was not likely to help her see around them. Lucy could only see herself and her experience from behind the same veil of thinking that told her to lay low and stay small. It was as if she wore a tight helmet of habitual, don't-mess-up thinking and she couldn't see herself from outside the helmet.

That's the thing about helmets—it doesn't take long to forget you're wearing one. Lucy no longer heard the conversation in her head. It was so habitual that it simply created her experience without Lucy realizing that it was just that—moving, changing *experience*. It looked to her like she was experiencing life as it was. She was the fish in water asking, "What's water?"

WHO-YOU-ARE AND WHAT YOU ARE NOT

You already are full of all the confidence, health, creativity, connection, and peace you could ever wish for. The only things that ever seem to get in the way are thoughts and feelings—psychological experience—that look like who-you-are, but aren't.

In the spirit of waking up to who-you-truly-are and living with peace of mind, free of self-doubt and insecurity, there are two things to see.

First, what you think, feel, and do doesn't mean anything about who-you-are. The habitual, insecure, ego-based, critical, me-me-me thoughts that run through your mind all day, every day, are not "you," and they are not "yours." They are the output of a machine brain. They are just what minds do.

The feelings those thoughts bring aren't you or yours either. The dread, pride, shame, desire to shrink, loneliness, smugness, or superiority…those are the felt part of thought. The felt part of what minds do. We feel thought. So, like thought, those feelings come and go. They are not lasting statements about who-you-are.

Our behavior follows from what we think and feel. Thoughts, feelings, and behavior make up our human psychology, and you are infinitely bigger than any passing-by psychology.

Second, who-you-are beyond your psychology is, well, words can't describe it. Your default, never-changing essence, is endless love, peace, and wisdom. It is endless confidence, creativity, resourcefulness, and common sense. Everything you ever wanted is who-you-are by nature, already. It's just temporarily hiding behind the psychology that's moving through.

You aren't insecure. Lucy wasn't either. You aren't a worrier. You aren't full of self-doubt, a shy person, an angry person, a resentful person. Our mind simply tells us we are these things, and we believe it.

Things like insecurity, worry, doubt, and anger are *psychological experiences,* not stable traits of human beings. They are labels that may characterize your in-this-moment experience, but they don't say a thing about *you.*

You might not believe this yet, but there's nothing wrong with you, no exceptions. You aren't lacking or broken. You are well as you are, in everything you may or may not be feeling, right this minute. The only reason you may not *feel* full of confidence, peace, and clarity is because you mistake what you think, feel, and do for who-you-are. We all do.

It's a simple misunderstanding. A clear-cut case of mistaken identity.

MY EXPERIENCE

I was asleep to who-I-am for most of my life.

From the time I was young, I was "a thinker," often lost in thought, trying to figure out how life worked. I worried a lot and carried the weight of the world on my shoulders.

All of that thinking took a toll on me. As a child, I had nightmares, twitches, and separation anxiety. My anxiety continued into adulthood and hit a peak in my midtwenties when I was having multiple panic attacks every day. I was afraid to leave my apartment, leaving only for necessities, for over a year.

I sought help for my anxiety, and it got better, but before I knew it, it showed up in new ways. My busy mind didn't endlessly worry about anything and everything anymore; instead, it chose one subject—food. I struggled with binge eating and bulimia, off and on, for eight years.

During that time I tried everything from traditional therapy to energy work, from hypnosis and meditation to willpower and discipline to end my habit. Everything I tried had only short-term impact, if any impact at all, because I didn't see my thoughts and feelings for what they were, and I didn't have a sense of who-I-was beyond my habit. My thoughts, feelings, and behaviors were always front and center in my experience, looking meaningful and problematic. Because I didn't understand my psychology, I thought I was mentally ill (as my frequent visits to psychologists would suggest). I thought I needed fixing. From that misunderstanding, it made sense to use effort and manipulation to try to change my experience. The only thing I knew to do was to fight, reframe, or distract myself from my experience. I didn't know there were other options.

Then, I came across the understanding I am sharing with you, and everything changed.

I learned that I was not my psychology at all. My thoughts, feelings, and behaviors—including my habits and anxieties—were not me. They were in constant motion, so how could they be me? They were always moving, coming and going beyond my control, so how could I be responsible for changing them?

I began to see that life actually worked the exact opposite of how I thought it worked. I couldn't be broken. I didn't need to be fixed, and neither did my experience—it just needed to be understood. Understanding provided a no-willpower way out.

When I saw how perfectly life worked, I was free. It took some time for my behavior to catch up with the freedom I knew was mine, but in a matter of weeks, my eight-year habit was a thing of the past. Anxiety, worry, and negative thinking haven't looked the same since. Even if they show up—which happens far less than it used to—they look like experience moving through, not a meaningful problem that I need to attend to, take personally, or fix.

HOW TO CLEAR UP
MISUNDERSTANDING

Change doesn't start with action.

Don't get me wrong—we take action along the way, but that's not where we want to start. Deep, lasting change starts with us waking up and seeing things in a way that we didn't see before. Behavior follows from there.

Consider growing up. As you've grown from, say, fifteen years old to the age you are today, life has looked different along the way. Your whole world view has evolved, and you didn't need willpower or effort to manage the change. As a natural result of growing up, the things that occur to you to do are different. You might like your music a little less loud. You probably spend less time obsessing about your clothing or fantasizing about your crushes. No one had to teach you to change in those ways. Your reality has changed, and your behaviors followed.

The same happens in all of life. When we see our psychology for what it is—moving, changing, energy flowing through us—and we become familiar with the unspeakable expansiveness that is beyond our psychology, everything begins to shift.

You're "waking up," rather than "learning," "doing," or "figuring out," because there is nothing you need that you don't already have. There is nothing to add, learn, or acquire, no willpower or effort needed. Waking up is subtractive. It's an unlearning—seeing that the thoughts, judgments, and opinions that have looked like "you" all this time, aren't.

You don't need self-help, you simply need to clear up some very simple misunderstandings and come to deeply realize that you are not your experience. You are not who you think you are

You will come to see that *what* you think and feel is not nearly as interesting as the fact *that* you think and feel—*that* thought and feeling make up your experience of life. It is life-changing to look toward how all humans work and concern yourself less with the specifics that appear so unique and personal to you.

YOUR MIND IS A KNOW-IT-ALL

Brains, and the minds with which they're linked, are prediction machines.

Your brain evolved to ensure your physical survival. The earliest humans who were fastest to predict potential threats in the environment—to hear a rustling in the bushes or sense the stare of a predator—were more likely to move to safety and pass on their prediction tendencies. To your brain, prediction equals security.

Consistent with its prognosticator role, your mind loves certainty. Knowing things, even before they happen, is how it does its job.

As you'll see throughout this book, evolution has turned your mind into a bit of a know-it-all. It works a little like the autocorrect feature on your smartphone, filling in blanks with guesses that are based on the past. It sacrifices accuracy when it does this, but that's okay to your brain. False positives are safer than not knowing, as far as your mind is concerned.

Minds don't love things that are new. They prefer familiar and predictable. New takes too much energy to figure out, and along with keeping you alive, your brain is an efficiency-loving machine. It has an enormous amount of work to do every moment of every day of your life, so it generalizes, extrapolates, and takes shortcuts wherever it can.

As know-it-alls, minds will try to take charge of everything, including our waking up to who-we-are.

Note that I could be saying *your* mind is efficient or *your* mind will try to take charge of your waking up. And sometimes I will. But I'll often say *minds* instead of *your mind* because I want you to see that this isn't personal. It's about *all* minds. All minds work in the same way. They're all up to the same tricks. Nothing here is about your mind versus your partner's mind, your kid's mind, or your friend's mind. It's about how all minds work.

So, a mind, your mind, all minds will try to take charge, but they can't help you wake up because you are already awake. It's only the mind's habitual stories that have us feeling asleep. When our mind falls quiet, we find what we've been looking for.

Given that your mind will try to take charge of things, and that all minds do this in a fairly universal way, here are some things your mind is likely to say along the way.

"I already know this."

A mind will swear that it already knows what you're reading here. Sometimes that might sound like, "I've heard this before, so I don't need to listen," or "She already said this" (to be fair, this book is repetitive, on purpose), or "This sounds like mindfulness/too spiritual for me/the same stuff so-and-so writes about."

Your mind might want to gloss over what you're hearing, keeping it conceptual and high-level, to save energy. Your mind isn't excited about you changing. Change is energy consuming and uncertain.

"This is too simple to be true."

The mind loves to show off how smart it is. It's expert in dealing with complexity and solving problems...or so it thinks. It's threatened by simplicity. Our mind worries, "If life is so simple, am I even needed?" Our mind would have us believe it's the sole reason we make it through the challenging, complicated world out there.

It's like learning to write HTML code only for drop and drag to become a thing. Or learning to do long division by hand, to graduate and be handed a calculator. The mind has a lot riding on life being complicated because it's the perfect tool for that job.

"But what about...?"

To your mind, nothing about you is simple, universal, or just like everyone else. You're as special and unique as they come.

Minds thrive on details, meaning, content, and story. Because they have such a hard time accepting simplicity, they'll balk at the suggestion that what we're exploring here is universal. They are excellent at arguing exceptions, and they'll claim to find them everywhere.

"Which is it…A or B?"

Minds are mechanical and computerlike. They are linear and logical. They think in black-and-white.

Life, and the truths we'll be exploring, is the complete opposite. Life does not unfold on a mind-created, linear line. Life is chock-full of gray area. Truth is bursting with paradox.

A linear, logical mind won't be afraid to let you know that it can't compute what doesn't follow conceptual rules. That's okay—you don't need it to.

"How am I doing?"

If you listen, you'll notice your mind evaluating…everything. Minds love to make up standards for you, convince you they're real, and then grade your progress. Minds love gold stars, and they're quick to let you know how well or how poorly you're doing. Your mind might even compare you to the people you read about in this book. Minds love to compare, it's just what minds do.

"I don't get it."

Yes, you do. Part of you is hearing something new and resonating with what you are hearing. But your mind wants to take control, and it will likely be confused.

It will hear paradox and gray area and things it can't compute. It will be baffled by the simplicity of things and demand to know where "you"—your mind-created identity—are in all of this.

Feeling a little disoriented, like you're in over your head, is perfect. You *are* "in over your head." That's the whole point. We're looking "over" your head, toward something bigger and truer. Let that feeling of confusion be a sign that your mind is busy at work, trying to get this for you. Let it be a reminder that your mind doesn't have an active role in waking up. You'll hear what's beyond the confusion as your mind relaxes.

The words in this book are only pointers toward what you already, deeply know.

So, while your mind will try to think its way through this book, I'm hoping for the opposite. With stories, a bit of repetition, and some no-thinking-required metaphors, I'm hoping to lull your analytical, smart mind to sleep.

My words and stories are aimed at the part of you that knows this already. That part of you will recognize these truths; don't worry.

When your mind is insisting that you aren't getting it, that it can't be this simple, that this is too vague, or that you know this already, come back to this: "I hear you, mind. But what if?"

What if life is this simple? (What if it's even simpler?)

What if you really are more healthy, creative, connected, confident, secure, and peaceful than you ever dreamed possible, right now, already?

What if the only thing that ever leads you to believe otherwise is a simple case of mistaken identity? A simple matter of thoughts and feelings (psychological experience) moving through you that look like "you" or "yours," but that truly are not?

Don't take my word for it, and please don't take your mind's word for it. This is a chance to set aside everything you think you already know about who you are and how life works, to look in a brand-new direction.

Just be open, curious, and willing to be impacted. If you can set aside your mind's commentary and come back to "What if this is true?" I know you'll be amazed at what you discover.

LUCY WAKES UP

Once Lucy saw herself and her experience in a new way, she realized a different reality was right under her nose the whole time.

How could it be that she was so much weaker or more failure-prone than others? Was she born this way? Were these deep, stable properties of who she was as a person? Lucy began to see that they weren't. She could remember a time when she wasn't so afraid, and she began to see present-day examples of peace and courage that she'd been blind to. She saw that it was only a ticker tape of fearful thoughts that distinguished her experience from that of her friends and coworkers.

For the first time ever, Lucy began to see other people make mistakes—sometimes big mistakes—more and more. She noticed that when others drew negative attention, they weren't ruined by it. In fact, sometimes their mistakes didn't seem to bother them at all.

If that was possible for them, wouldn't it have to be possible for Lucy too?

Lucy remembered how baffled people were by her timidity. Throughout her life, people wondered what she was so worried about, why she was so serious, why she didn't date more, why she couldn't see herself the way they saw her. People told her how kind and funny she was "once we get to know you." Before, Lucy's mind couldn't let these inquires and compliments in. They were so far outside of what she believed that her mind filtered them out or came up with reasons they weren't relevant. ("She says that about everyone.") Now, more often than not, Lucy is curious about others' opinions of her. How could it be that they see her so differently than she sees herself? What if their impressions are more accurate than her own?

Lucy saw that her mind-made comfort zone never provided safety or comfort. It kept her world small and reinforced her irrational fears.

Little by little, Lucy noticed her mind fall quiet. She had growing glimpses of what life felt like when she wasn't thinking about herself and her limitations. There were brief moments when she forgot she was an insecure, worried mess. Those moments were bliss.

She began to see beyond the identity her mind created. She began to gradually see around the habitual thoughts and feelings that had looked like who-she-was for so long.

Lucy asked, "Doesn't the fact that my mind is always creating this identity, doling out these warnings and fears, mean there must be something to them? Why else would my mind go there so often?"

"What if it's just the opposite?" I asked back. "If fear and insecurity are innately, deeply who-you-are, why would your mind need to remind you all the time? Your mind doesn't go around repeating other 'truths' to you, does it? It doesn't need to remind you all the time what your name is or how gravity works.

"Your mind is a habitual, repetitive machine. What if these thoughts and feelings are just the workings of that machine? They seem pretty mechanical, don't they?"

As she saw beyond what she had always believed, she was blown away. Had this whole "insecure Lucy" thing really been a mind-created identity that was never as true or solid as it appeared? Could it be nothing more than the result of some simple misunderstandings about who-she-was and how minds work?

It's like when you're in a dark movie theater, in one of those comfy, reclining seats, fully engrossed in the film. Your heart is pumping in sync with the main character's heart as he walks down the dark alley. You're stepping his every step, looking around all the same ominous corners. "Movie" is nowhere in your consciousness. Racing heart and dark alley is the only reality you know.

And then, a cell phone in the pocket of a fellow theater patron buzzes, and the illusion is disrupted. You are now in a theater, watching a movie. Nothing in the world has changed, but everything about your experience has.

This is how it was for Lucy. It's how it was for me, and how it's been for so many others.

We wake up. And like one of those hidden picture puzzles, once we see the hidden figure, we can't un-see it. It is clear and obvious, and we can't believe we missed it before.

We're all Lucy. We've all gone through life believing our habitual thoughts and feelings.

When we wake up, we realize that who-we-really-are has been there all along.

PART I

MEET YOUR
MIND

1. The Mind That Never Stops Thinking

There is a voice in your head that never stops talking. I bet you've noticed.

It's the one with opinions about everything. It tells you what it likes and dislikes, what's good and bad, what's acceptable and intolerable, how you're better or worse than others, how you're too old, too young, too quiet, too loud, too, too, too...

It's the voice that loves categories, descriptions, words, and identities. It's like a label-maker, creating and slapping labels on everything it perceives.

It's the voice that offers a second-by-second play-by-play of everything going on within and around you. When your alarm clock goes off in the morning, it says, "Five-thirty already? Time to get up." You're already up. You already heard the alarm and saw the time. The voice isn't giving you brand-new information, it's just offering a chronicle of events that's redundant, yet oddly comforting.

As you stumble from your bed to the bathroom, your mind replays the dreams you just had, goes through a list of what's on tap for the day, criticizes you for that dumb thing you said yesterday. It looks at you in the mirror and says your hair is thinning, your wrinkles are showing, your eyebrows need plucking.

The inner narrator is obsessed with time. It loves talking about the past and the future. Yesterday, today, and tomorrow. Before, later, someday.

It's dramatic. It exaggerates like crazy and then claims it's not exaggerating at all. Most of what it reports is full of colorful commentary. He shoots, he scores! The crowd erupts into a roar as they jump to their feet! The inner narrator—your mind—adds story, meaning, and feeling to everything. When your mind is talking (and it always is), things don't just happen—they happen with energy and emotion, in full color, high-definition, with the best special effects. Life unfolds with backstory and dramatic detail, as a meaningful multidimensional experience.

In direct and indirect ways, the voice, your mind, relates everything to you. You're the center of its universe. "Did you see that fight between James and Ann in the break room yesterday? My coworkers are crazy," your mind will say. "They make me look good." Or, "What kind place is this? Maybe I should put out feelers for a new job." Most of what your mind talks about—and pretty much all that it cares about—has you at the center.

Although the narrator is linear and black-or-white, it contradicts itself all the time. It says, "You're having a rough day; you deserve a long nap." When you wake up, it says, "I can't believe you took a nap in the middle of the day. What's wrong with you?"

It goes from one extreme to the other. It tells you you're not good enough, no one likes you, you should just stay quiet because no one wants to hear from you. It will look to past experience to prove that it's right. Minutes later, it will give you a pep talk full of suggestions for how to improve. "Maybe you should learn a new language. Be funnier. Try to be more relevant." Later that same day, it's imagining you as the confident, secure life of the party. "Just listen to me," your mind seems to say, "and everything will turn out okay. I'll help you get what you want." It is the creator of your problems and the wannabe problem solver.

The voice is loud and opinionated, but perhaps its best trick is turning itself invisible. One minute, it will make sure you know that it's responsible for everything good that's ever happened. ("You've made it this far in life because of your smart, hardworking mind, you know.") The next minute, it goes rogue and pretends it doesn't exist. It'll convince you that your moment-to-moment experience is coming from life "out there," that there is an "out there" that is totally independent of your mind. As the physicist David Bohm said, "Thought creates our world and then says, 'I didn't do it.'" Your mind creates your experience through thought and feeling, at the same time making it appear that the dog getting sick on your white rug is what made you grumpy or today being Friday is what has you so happy.

Sometimes the voice appears to fall silent. Have you noticed how different life looks and feels when the voice isn't talking so much? Life seems brighter, richer, and more vivid. Time slows down, and experience is heightened. Nothing is different on the outside, but everything *feels* different, the way you notice how a delicious meal tastes when you slow down to enjoy it.

Other times, your mind is racing, like you're wearing a helmet full of fast, urgent thoughts. Your mind is shouting words like "now!" and "must!" Life is full of problems that must be solved immediately. Opinions are exaggerated and feel truer than ever. Life feels very personal—everything your mind says is about what could go wrong *for you*.

I often use a pair of those wind-up, plastic, chattering teeth to illustrate how our mind—the narrator—seems to work. You know the chattering teeth, right? Bright red plastic gums and tall, shiny white teeth. You wind them up, and they chatter and chomp around your table.

Everyone knows the feeling of a mind going on and on, wound up, chattering about everything and nothing until it runs out of juice. The teeth put on a dramatic show, but they are a hunk of plastic, all wound up.

The chattering teeth convey a certain disrespect that I think is hilarious and immensely helpful. It's never a problem that we think a lot, that we get wound up, or that our mind works the way it does. Things only feel problematic for us when we take the mind seriously. When we confuse ourselves—who-we-truly-are—with that piece of cheap, chattering plastic.

The chattering teeth are a little mechanical device doing what it's designed to do.

So is your mind.

* * *

See if you can notice your narrator from time to time today. Can you see how repetitive, opinionated, and almost mechanical it sounds?

2. How It Begins

There once was a baby named Willow.

Willow was born into a loud room with florescent lights. The midwife labeled her "girl" and "healthy" and handed her to the person they called "mother."

The baby's parents name her Willow, but Willow won't know herself as Willow for many months. When she does learn to respond to that label, who knows what she'll make of it? She doesn't know what a Willow is, what a mother, father, dog, or diaper are. Words and labels lump and define. Nothing in Willow's experience is lumped or defined yet. Imagine the most unbound, open, free oneness you've ever felt, and multiply that by infinity. I imagine that's what Willow knew before her birth into physical form, and something close to that is what she still knows before her mind learns to comprehend words and labels.

You feel that enormous oneness when you look deep into her blue, baby eyes. She's the entire universe crammed into eight pounds of adorable fat and wrinkly baby skin.

This newly born baby is as connected as can be with the pure consciousness that is who-she-is. Her narrator hasn't shown up yet, so there's no constant talking, categorizing, or meaning making. There's just one, universal category: This. Here. Now. Is.

As Willow grows and her brain develops, she becomes smart. She learns with amazing speed. She responds to her name and begins calling people and objects by their names. She knows what she likes—her stuffed bunny Hoppy, mashed avocado, watching her parents try to keep her two Yorkies from licking her chubby baby hands—and what she dislikes—sleeping in her crib, wet diapers, sudden loud noises.

Willow's world is filling with divisions and concepts, but it's still a huge, safe world. She doesn't cling to the meaning and preferences passing through. Thought and feeling move through her like clouds move through the sky. Willow feels them while they're there, and naturally lets them fall away as they leave. It doesn't occur to her that her experience belongs to her in any way. There isn't a solid "her" to which they might belong.

As Willow grows older, her narrator mind is expanding its vocabulary. By two or three years old, there is a distinct, solid-seeming "Willow" who possesses things, which she lets us know with the now-popular words "me" and "mine." She's vaguely aware of the concepts "past" and "future," although she still doesn't leave the present much. When a family friend asks, "Are you excited to start preschool in the fall?" her face lights up as she says "Yes!" and then she instantly returns to the toys right in front of her.

At three or four years old, Willow's imagination is through the roof. She hosts incredible birthday parties for her stuffed animals where they play games and eat outrageous foods. Her mind is becoming more skilled at making things up, and she falls into those imaginary ideas as if they were absolutely true. She regularly loses sight of the distinction between what is "real" in the physical world around her and what her mind creates. There is a fine line between Willow's thoughts and what feels true.

Little by little, as Willow's brain develops, she's pulled away from the present moment and into her head. This trend will continue gradually. It will happen in a more pronounced way at times too, like when something scary happens.

Something scary eventually happens to all of us. I'm not talking about being afraid of the dark or hearing a ghost story—this something scary feels personal. It shakes our foundation and threatens our sense of who we think we are and how life needs to be for us to be okay. It's often one of our earliest traumatic memories.

For far too many people, it's abuse. For others, it's being teased by the neighbor kid and feeling shame for the first time. Or being disapproved of by an adult and feeling not good enough for the first time. For me, it was my parents fighting and feeling my sense of security threatened for the first time.

The event itself, although sometimes horribly distressing, isn't the point. What leads us into our heads is that our mind makes the event about us in some way. It's not just that *the event* was not okay; it's that *we* are not okay. If we want to feel safe and secure again (and of course we do, nothing is more important), we better find a way to protect ourselves.

But we're kids. Who is coming to the rescue? The narrator, of course. The narrator is waiting in the wings, armed with solutions so we never have to feel this horrible feeling again. It'll help us feel secure in the world, the way we did before this scary thing happened.

If the neighbor kid teased you for being too weak, your mind hatches a plan. You'll be so tough that they'll never call you weak again. You'll show no vulnerability.

If your parents are breaking up and you're caught in the cross-fire, you'll be perfect. You'll be so flawless they couldn't forget about you if they tried. You'll be so good the breakup couldn't possibly be your fault.

If you were abused, you'll shrink. You'll go inward, stay so small they can't find you. Or maybe you'll lash out. You'll be so tough they'll never hurt you again. Your mind's primary job is your survival. One of the ways it does its job is by crafting a solid identity, a "you," that allows you to know who-you-are, complete with a host of protective mechanisms to keep your made-up identity safe and secure. Since that scary thing happened, your mind is hard at work determining who-you-are and who you need to be in order to survive.

And just like that, over several short years, our expansive, universe-in-a-body baby begins to think of herself as an individual with a name and a collection of traits and strategies to keep her safe. She goes from living in the present moment to often living in her head. She goes from living by moment-to-moment wisdom to consulting her narrator and its master plan.

She goes from being fluid, letting thought and feeling pass through freely—naturally crying and then stopping, playing and then resting—to being vigilant. To looking at experience as if it were meaningful and personal, assessing whether it's safe or dangerous. She holds her sense of "me" in mind as something solid she can always rely upon.

Of course, more scary things happen throughout her life. The more complex and fragile her identity is, the more her security appears to be at risk, requiring even more strategies to be formed and carried through time.

It doesn't take long for our little human to forget that her mind created these plans and identities. She forgets that a scared, hurting, little kid's mind made them up. They begin to look like who-she-is, her personality. She says, "This is how I'm wired," or "This is how I've always been."

It's not how she's always been, but she forgets.

We think this is who-we-are.

* * *

Can you see how you gradually came to live more in your head, and less in life, as you grew up?

What if living in your mind-created identities and strategies is not as helpful or natural as it seems?

3. Who You Think You Are

Have you noticed that almost everything you think is about "you"?

This thing called "me" is the reference point for most of our thoughts. It's *your* body and *your* mind. They're *your* thoughts, *your* feelings, *your* habits, and *your* experiences. Your mind thinks about how *your* day might go. It talks about how to get ahead in *your* career, raise *your* children, and plan for *your* future.

To your mind, "you" are the center of the universe. Everything revolves around you.

Given the me-centricity of the mind, what I'm about to propose might sound crazy, but here goes.

What if there is no "you"?

What if the "me" identity that's been subtly evolving your entire life—full of traits, labels, characteristics, memories, and preferences—that feels so matter-of-fact, is simply a by-product of the way your brain works?

It's what minds do. They create thought about a seemingly stable "you" that's so timeworn, familiar, and convincing that we don't realize our mind made it up. It feels so real that our mind refers back to it nonstop throughout life.

This can be a difficult idea to consider particularly for those of us in Western culture, where we're conditioned to view thought, intellect, and rationalism as paramount. Our philosophies, religions, and sciences have focused on the mind and its physical counterpart, the brain, as the center of who-we-are. As a result, the idea of an independent-from-others, brain-centered "me" reigns supreme.

But it's helpful to remember that in Eastern traditions, like Buddhism and Taoism, the idea that there is no "you" is commonplace. One of the most fundamental tenants in Buddhism—*anatta*—translates to "no self." The Tao Te Ching calls the idea of a separate self a "compelling illusion." We all *experience* an entity we call "me." But an illusion is something created by the mind, without an independent existence in the physical world. That's the view of the self I'm suggesting. One that's more verb than noun, created by thought in each and every moment.

Like baby Willow, we're born into an experience of consciousness that is infinitely open and expansive. As our brain develops language and storytelling abilities, it begins naming things. That's mommy, different from daddy. That's dog, separate from brother. Eventually, this is me, separate from you, him, her, and them.

The brain loves to categorize, classify, label, and name because it loves certainty. Knowing things about the world around you, and knowing "you," is how the brain fulfills its primary mission—to help you survive. The more it knows, the more it can predict. The more it can predict, the more it can prevent anything that might pose a threat to your survival. The brain is designed for this. When life is uncertain or something scary happens that appears to threaten "you," the narrator mind jumps in with a story that not only makes sense of things, it calms us into believing it has a plan for the future that will keep us safe. In the very big picture, predicting things with confidence was adaptive. It was better for early human brains to sacrifice accuracy for a plan. If a brain predicted that a rival tribe was around the corner and it was, the result was survival. If a brain made the same prediction but was wrong, a little energy may have been wasted, but nothing worse than that. False positives are favored over false negatives when we're facing actual threats. In today's world, without physical threats around every corner, our false positives are less helpful.

Research in cognitive and social psychology, and neuroscience, illustrates how our brain works to create what we think of as "me."[*] Our mind loves certainty so much that it fabricates reasons and stories to give us a sense of certainty. In one well-known study, in which women were asked to inspect several samples of pantyhose and choose the highest quality pair, they gave all sorts of detailed reasons for their choice. They said the pantyhose they chose were thicker, felt like they were more durable and better made. The women didn't hesitate to tell the researchers exactly why their chosen pantyhose were better than the others. While the reasons

---

[*]   Chris Niebauer (2019) has written an entire book that expands on some of the research mentioned in this chapter. If you want a much more thorough treatment of the neuropsychology, I highly recommend his book *No Self, No Problem: How Neuropsychology Is Catching Up to Buddhism.*

they provided made logical sense, they were inaccurate. All the pantyhose in the study were the same. Our mind is happy to make a choice and provide compelling reasons for that choice with little regard for accuracy (Nisbett and Wilson 1977).

The left brain, often called "the interpreter," is responsible for making sense of the sensory information the brain takes in. It uses language to fill in blanks, connect dots, and tell stories that appear logical and provide a sense of certainty, even if it is totally wrong.

Some of the most fascinating studies on how the left brain tells untrue stories have been done on split-brain patients. Split-brain patients are people who have had the corpus callosum, the brain matter connecting the right and left hemispheres, severed (often as a last resort attempt to control severe epilepsy). With a severed corpus callosum, the right and left hemispheres are unable to communicate with each other, which is troublesome in many ways for the patient, but allows researchers to study the unique roles of the right and left hemispheres in a way they can't in those of us with a connected brain.

In one of these studies, patients were shown a card that said the word "laugh," seen only by their left visual field. Because we are cross-wired—our left hemisphere controls the right side of our body and vice versa—and because the card was shown to the left visual field and the two sides of the brain don't communicate with each other in these patients, the card was only seen by the right side of the brain.

Following directions, the patient laughed when their right brain saw the card that said "laugh." When they were asked why they were laughing, the left hemisphere, where language and reasoning live, was as quick to provide a plausible, but wrong explanation like, "I just thought of a funny memory." Like in the pantyhose study, the explanation was dead wrong, but the left-brain storyteller provided explanations with speed and confidence (Gazzaniga 1985).

There are volumes of research showing that the mind is a storyteller and its stories are wrong.

Because your brain has the most important job of keeping you alive, and because the world looks very complex to your brain, it loves efficiency. It takes shortcuts anywhere it can. The generalizing part of the left brain takes in brushstrokes of paint on a canvas and gives you an experience of Monet's *Water Lily Pond*. It takes in combinations of letters and abstracts the ideas in this book. It's always looking to extract patterns and meaning from sensory information, which is amazing for your ability to appreciate art or read a book, but is less ideal when your brain is thinking about the mistake you made at work today and generalizes that into a convincing picture of you as "the kind of person" who isn't good enough at their job.

Minds generalize as far as they can to get the most information and predictive value for their effort. So, not only did you make a mistake today, you're likely to make another one tomorrow. Come to think of it, you're likely to fall short in other areas of life too.

Confirmation bias is one example of how a mind tends to search for, interpret, and more easily remember information that confirms our existing beliefs. This is how a single thought in a single moment (e.g., I made a mistake today) brings to mind a flood of supporting evidence. It's how a single thought in a single moment becomes a seemingly meaningful statement about who-you-are as a person, made subconsciously in an instant (Nickerson 1998).

Our categorizing, generalizing left hemisphere also houses the language center of the brain, which makes perfect sense given that language is a categorization system full of labels and symbols. Language cannot possibly communicate objective truth because language itself is symbolic. But as fish in water with our own thinking, we naturally and often mistake the map for the territory (Korzybski 1933). We take the narrator's constant talking about "me" at face value, but it's really representations and symbols. It's a conversation that's not necessarily all that accurate, as we've seen. Our "me"-ness—the traits, qualities, strengths, weaknesses, labels, and roles—is a generalized, conceptualized, blanks-filled-in, highly inaccurate conversation that we assume tells the truth of who-we-are.

Are you beginning to see how "I" is no different from any thought arising from the mind? "I" and "me" are stories too, and they are the ones with the highest stakes. "You" are the subject your brain is most motivated to know, since "you" are what it's trying to keep alive. When we take what the brain tells us as the truth of who-we-are and it looks as if there is a stable "me," we naturally find ourselves defending and protecting that identity. We go out of our way to keep our idea of ourselves safe, which leads us to avoid things that might lead to "failure," to be sensitive to others' opinions about who-we-are, or to avoid uncomfortable feelings that seem like "ours." Our world becomes small.

My favorite illustration of how our sense of self is a function of the brain is the experience of Jill Bolte Taylor (2006) after she experienced a left-hemisphere stroke. You may be familiar with her incredible book, *My Stroke of Insight.*

Bolte Taylor's stroke left her brain unable to carry out its typical labeling, judging, storytelling, dot-connecting, pattern-creating, and "me" referencing. She describes an experience reminiscent of baby Willow's experience before her left-brain interpreter came online. She describes living in the most incredible expansiveness and oneness with everyone and everything. Without an active narrator highlighting "me," "mine," "them," and "theirs," the boundaries between herself and the rest of the world faded. There was no linear past and future, there was only now. Without a left-brain label-maker, life was a fluid ebb and flow of experience, rather than a parade of solid-looking objects and concepts.

My Stroke of Insight was a life-changing book for me. Jill Bolte Taylor's experience deeply landed as a perfect illustration of who we are *beyond* the mind and brain, and who we think we are *because of* the mind and brain. The expansiveness, the connection, the oneness, the love, peace, and clarity...those are the always-there, undamageable essence of who-we-are. The rest is mental activity creating an amazing illusory self that we mistake for who-we-are.

Let me be clear that our solid-seeming sense of self is not a bad thing. It's not a mistake or a misguided function of the brain. There are no misguided functions of the brain, only misunderstood ones.

Having a sense of ourselves as real and independent from the rest of the world is an incredible gift. It makes the game of life fun. It gives us the experience of growth and evolution, winning and losing, happiness and sadness. It makes way for a life experience that is so engaging, in part because it feels so personal. Without a "me" character playing this game, life would be completely different.

But imagine playing this realistic, seemingly high-stakes, full-of-variety game as "you," knowing it's a game.

Imagine playing the game of life with the understanding that the security and happiness your character is trying desperately to nail down isn't actually at risk. Security and contentment are what's there beyond your mind talking about what you lack. They can't be lost. At worst, they are temporarily hidden from view, "talked over" by your mind.

It matters that the self is a convincing illusion, as the Buddha said, because 100 percent of our suffering is rooted in the idea of there being a stable "me" that can be hurt or damaged. When we think there is a "me" who needs protection, we protect it. Our mind makes up rules and limitations and avoids things that feel threatening. Our world looks dangerous and becomes small, all in the name of protecting something that doesn't even exist. It's an innocent misunderstanding of a well-working left brain.

Taoist philosopher Wei Wu Wei said it best: "Why are you unhappy? Because 99.9 percent of everything you think, and of everything you do, is for yourself—and there isn't one."

* * *

What if, in the name of certainty and therefore survival, brains make stuff up and pass it off as truth?

What would that mean for how seriously we take our own thoughts?

4. Who-You-Are

If we aren't who we *think* we are, who are we? I can't answer that for you. I can't even answer it for myself. But my left brain will use some language to point in a direction that I hope opens up your own exploration.

In my limited left-brain words, we are the expansive pure consciousness we were born into, before so much was added and learned. We're the Golden Buddha. Do you know about the Golden Buddha?

Somewhere around the thirteenth century in Bangkok, Thailand, a massive statue of the Buddha was made of pure gold.

Not long after the statue was created, Burmese soldiers invaded Thailand. In a flash of insight, the Thai people covered the Golden Buddha in stucco and glass to hide its value and keep it safe from the invaders. Who would want a huge, heavy Buddha statue made of sand and dirt?

The invaders came and went, and the statue was spared. The few people who knew the true nature of the Golden Buddha eventually died. Then, in the 1960s when the statue was being moved from one temple to another, it was dropped. The plaster cracked, and a pure gold toe shined through Buddha's dirty façade. The crack in the façade meant the jig was up. The Golden Buddha's shiny, perfect nature was realized.

When that scary thing happened and you retreated into your head, your mind created a façade to keep you safe. Your mind told you the kind of person you were, and the way you needed to be from then forward to be accepted and safe. Because those strategies and the façade felt like safety, you looked toward and identified with them more and more, and you looked toward and identified with your true nature less and less. The psychological experience moving through you took center stage and your expansive, nonverbal essence fell to the background. You slowly but surely mistook fleeting thoughts, feelings, and behaviors for who-you-are.

You slowly but surely fell asleep to your true nature.

But nothing about who-you-are has ever changed. You're as peaceful and connected to all of life as you've always been. You've simply gotten into the habit of listening to your mind a little too closely. We listen so closely to the narrator, our conditioned, habitual, machinelike mind, that it becomes all we hear.

And then, one day, you get dropped. You go through a breakup or a breakdown. You find yourself anxious, sick, or with an addiction you can't kick. You lose your job. You can't get pregnant. Or you can, but your kids grow up, and you no longer recognize who you thought you were.

You get dropped, and you're unable to pick yourself up and go back to how things were, which is excellent news. You're dropped so hard a crack is formed, and you're forced to look beyond the appearance of things. You catch a glimpse of what's there beyond the façade.

Insights into who-you-are don't require an identity crisis, that's just one opportunity to look deeper. Insights into who-you-are can come from openness and curiosity, a willingness to look beyond surface-level appearances and not take your moment-to-moment thoughts as truth. It takes a willingness to look toward something with which you are deeply acquainted, but also unaware. You are willing or you wouldn't be reading this book.

No one can see it for you. The only thing other people can do is share their experiences and insights. All I can do is write about how I see it, tell you stories, share some science, and give you some metaphors about chattering teeth and Golden Buddhas. But all of my words are just pointers, pointing you back toward what you might see for yourself, from beyond your own chatty, doubting mind. To get any personal impact, you need to follow the pointers and explore this for yourself.

When I initially came across the understanding I'm sharing here, my teacher would give me his own pointers. He'd say things like "get quiet," "look within," "fall out of your thinking," and "go beyond your conceptual mind."

So, I'd sit in silence, looking somewhere that felt like "within," except I wasn't discovering anything because I was looking with my mind, and minds are too smart to discover. I was *mentally focusing on* the space within, *thinking about* it. That's not discovery, it's confirmation. It was me staying in my head, thinking about what I thought I should be exploring. That's the way a smart adult would go about discovery, but you want to do it the way a newborn baby would, guided by curiosity and not-knowing rather than by expectations and assumptions.

The essence of you that never changes is so close that you can't possibly think your way there. As soon as you engage your intellect, you're moving in the wrong direction.

I can't tell you how many times I've been in a group where we close our eyes, get quiet, and fall out of our thinking for just a minute or two, and a handful of people deeply sense themselves beyond their thinking. They're blown away at how still and beautiful and *close* it is. They sob. Or they sit in amazement that "This has been right there, so close, this whole time?"

When my kids were four or five years old, I'd say something like, "When you're warm and cozy in your bed, and you're just starting to get really sleepy...you know how there's a really nice, peaceful feeling there as your mind falls asleep, right before the rest of you falls asleep?"

Yes, they knew it.

"That's you. That's the exact same you that you were as a tiny baby, the part that will never change even as you grow up and turn into an old lady or an old man. It will always be right there, beneath your thoughts and feelings. Even when you can't feel it, it's there because it's you."

My kids were familiar with who-they-are when they were just four years old. I recently shared this with my daughter's Girl Scout troop, a room of nine- and ten-year-old girls, and they knew it too.

It's my more mature students who claim to forget, but even they sense it with a reminder or two. We've all felt overwhelmed with love, a sense of oneness with nature, or deep, quiet peace. We simply don't realize that what we're feeling is who-we-are, our default nature, so we give the credit to something outside of us, like the people we're with or the beautiful sunset.

Explore that pre-thought, pre-verbal space yourself. See if you can sense the still, deep peace that's there. The more you recognize that space as you, the closer and more familiar it feels.

But you have to promise me one thing.

You have to promise me that you won't believe your mind if it starts hassling you about *not* feeling that quiet, peaceful place right away.

If you look within and you don't feel what your mind thinks you should feel, please don't make anything of that. Your mind will tell stories. It's just trying to own this experience and do this for you, but remember, it's not needed here.

Given what minds do, yours has probably been painting a picture of how your exploration should look and feel throughout this entire chapter. It's been coming up with standards against which to judge your progress so you can decide whether you believe me or not or whether you pass or fail this exploration. Your mind is on standby to tell a shame-filled story about what it means if you don't have the "look within" experience you think you should.

That's just what minds do.

Please don't take it seriously. You can't fail at exploring who-you-are. Only a mind would tell you otherwise.

* * *

What if exploring who-you-are beyond your psychology is as natural as falling asleep at night? What if everything you've been looking for naturally *finds you* when your mind falls quiet?

Just Another Thought

What if the space beyond your habitual thinking feels uncomfortable?

Visit my website, https://www.dramy johnson.com/justathought, to watch a video of me speaking on this and other topics.

5. You Aren't Insecure, You Just Think You Are

Sydney Banks was as ordinary as they come.

He was a Scottish man living in British Columbia, Canada, married with two children, working as a welder. Although he had some interest in spiritual topics, he was no spiritual scholar. He was an ordinary man, living an ordinary life.

In 1973, Syd and his wife Barbara went to a workshop in the hopes of improving their relationship. While there, Syd became friendly with another participant in the workshop. The two men bonded over the fact that they both struggled with insecurity.

Syd Banks saw his friend later in the weekend, and as Syd tells it, the man said, "You know, Syd, the other night you told me you were insecure, and I've never heard such nonsense in all my life."**

Syd heard something far beyond the words his new friend said.

He heard in his simple words that there is no such thing as insecurity, there is only insecure thought. In that moment, Syd knew that *he* was not insecure, he only *thought* he was.

Exactly.

** You can watch Sydney Banks tell this story himself here: https://www .youtube.com/watch?v=p8ICFLZCNXc. Please do. It's far better than my rendition.

In each and every moment, we feel the thought moving through us, the thought and feeling we're identified with, mistaking for truth.

The man's words were a pointer that catapulted Sydney Banks far beyond intellect, labels, and psychology. The offhand comment put a crack in the façade of who Syd thought he was. That crack was the beginning of a massive awakening.

Syd didn't sleep for three days. He deeply saw who we all are, beyond our thought-created experience. Sydney Banks went on to share his enlightenment experience with people around the world for the next thirty-five years of his life. His realizations are often referred to as the Three Principles, and his teachings have been an enormous influence in my life and on everything shared in this book.

This is as true for you, as it was for Syd, as it is for all of us. You aren't insecure, you just think you are.

You aren't critical or judgmental when critical and judgmental thoughts move through you. Your experience doesn't make you a critical or judgmental person. Thought and feeling move through, and we innocently identify with them. We assume it's personal because they're showing up in our experience. But it isn't personal.

You aren't anxious, depressed, fearful. You aren't extraverted, disorganized, neurotic. You don't have an addictive personality, you aren't a procrastinator, perfectionist, or self-saboteur. You just *think* you are.

Literally.

You don't exhibit these traits all the time. If you look closely, you'll see that even your most prominent characteristics and personality traits—that shyness, indecisiveness, insecurity, assertiveness—are nowhere to be found for periods of time every single day. The most assertive person on earth isn't always. The most indecisive person you know makes quick and clear decisions at times. These things are not as fixed or constant as your mind tells you they are.

As we've seen, minds generalize. Your brain's job is to know stuff, so it can predict stuff, so you can survive longer. What could be more important for your mind to know than who-you-are? That linear, logical machine in your head is invested in you having a stable, count-on-able personality.

Once your mind decides you're anxious, for example, confirmation bias kicks in, and you see proof of it everywhere. Of course, plenty of nonanxious experience moves through you as well, but you miss it, dismiss it, or consider it a fluke.

And so, anxious experience repeats itself. Not because it is who-you-are, but because *you think* it's who-you-are. Your mind seeks to validate its experiences to bolster the identity it's creating for you. It seeks to validate its experiences to create a sense of safety.

At best, "I am anxious" is a summary of how experience *tends to* show up. And it's a summary statement that is full of exceptions.

Of course we look at the stuff that arises within us most often and think it's us. Experience has an "isness" that our true, expansive nature doesn't have. It has boundaries and names. Our mind can recognize it, and we have a language for it. It looks solid and real, so it's no wonder we identify with it.

It's no wonder we look at a thought, feeling, or memory, moving through wide open consciousness, and say, "Hello there. You must be me."

* * *

What would it mean for your life today if the traits and tendencies you've identified with over the years are far more fluid, and far less about "you," than they've seemed?

6. Hannah

Hannah came to me for help with her eating disorder.

She was in her midtwenties, sensitive, and exceptionally thoughtful. Hannah had an energy that made people want to be around her. She was a second-grade teacher who loved her work. Her students adored "Miss Hannah."

When I met Hannah, she had just purchased her first home, a one-bedroom condo in a suburb of San Francisco. She'd lose herself in decorating magazines and home design shows, bathing in creative ideas she could bring to life in her own home.

Without realizing it, Hannah had a lot of thoughts about how her life should look, and her mind created all sorts of rules to fulfill those expectations. Everything good in Hannah's life—and there was plenty—was at risk of going away at any moment...so her mind told her anyway. If her mind didn't stay constantly vigilant, predicting disasters and rehearsing what might go wrong, everything would fall apart.

When Hannah took her narrator's rules as truth, she felt overwhelming anxiety. She thought the fear and sense of not measuring up were coming from actual demands on her. From whom or where, she didn't know. It wasn't logical, but it felt so real that it must be true. She took the pressure and anxiety as evidence that she wasn't doing life the way she should.

The cycle of fear and judgment that Hannah's mind kept her in became unbearable. The more she felt it, the more personal it seemed. She began to stuff the panic down with food. When the fear and judgment *plus* all of that unacceptable food in her body was unbearable, she began to throw it all up.

Hannah and I had our video calls first thing on Monday mornings. One particular Monday, Hannah was in a tailspin about a recent binge.

She looked exhausted and sheepish, refusing to hold my gaze for more than a few seconds. She looked at her lap, her hands, out the window. She talked fast about everything she had eaten over the weekend. She talked about all the ways she had tried to purge, exercise, and starve to counteract her actions. She recounted the many trips to the grocery store and how she assaulted herself along the way.

She said she knew what to do—just don't follow through on her urges to eat. So why couldn't she do that? She said she was weak and nowhere near good enough.

Hannah said she was bloated and starving at the same time. She estimated how many calories she had taken in and how many she could still expel, as if she could really know such a thing. Her eyes, still not catching mine, darted back and forth as her mind did the math. She squirmed in her too-tight jeans as she calculated the weight of the weekend.

Her eyes pooled with tears that dripped onto her keyboard, and it was shockingly simple and obvious to me. These were not Hannah's thoughts.

They were passing through her mind, and the words were coming from her mouth, but Hannah—the real Hannah—the thoughtful, creative woman I knew, didn't care this much about calories, weight, or the way her pants fit.

No way.

This was the same laundry list of concerns I always heard from Hannah and from virtually everyone whose mind chose food and weight as its favorite fixation. They were the same thoughts that ran through my mind when I was caught up in that habit. There was nothing unique about them.

The frantic back-and-forth of what's wrong with me, and I can't believe, and not again, and what if—and the deep shame and hopelessness that was coming out of Hannah's mouth—was not her. It was the monotonous output of a conditioned machine. Hannah, herself, was not genuinely obsessed with any of this.

You know those energy-saving, motion-detecting lights they have in office buildings and freezer aisles at the grocery store, that turn on when someone walks into the room? It would be like you thinking the lights were coming on because of you. I mean, they are coming on because a body—maybe yours—is in the vicinity. But the lights aren't about you. They aren't a sign that you should buy what's in the freezer. They are simply a machine working the way it was designed to work.

That's how Hannah's mind was working. It was spinning on boring, old, repetitive topics it cared about, while Hannah thought *she* was the one who cared.

She thought that because she felt such deep dread at the thought of gaining weight, gaining weight must be authentically important to her.

Because her mind tracked calories and exercise and numbers on a scale to the extent that it did, and because those activities were tied to the highest of highs and the lowest of lows, this obsession must be "hers."

But, it wasn't. There was another explanation.

Hannah's black-and-white, rule-based, habitual, computer mind was having the same conversation it had thousands of times before. It was a conversation that was familiar, efficient, and seemingly helpful to Hannah's brain. And kind, wise, innately healthy Hannah was simply caught up in a case of mistaken identity.

As Hannah became curious about who she was beyond her mind's habitual thoughts and feelings, she sensed a space that became increasingly familiar. She felt her way toward that quiet, peaceful place where she didn't feel any pressure to be different. In that space, as witness to her experience, she watched the identity named Hannah experience expectations and rules and urges to numb from it all, but with some distance, she saw how safe and impersonal it truly was.

* * *

What if the habitual thoughts that move through you aren't necessarily reflective of your true desires, opinions, or preferences? Can you sense the freedom in that?

7. Untouchable

A classic metaphor for who-you-are and how your human experience works is the sky and weather.

It goes like this. Who-you-are is like the clear blue sky. And your experience—your moment-to-moment thoughts, feelings, cravings, desires, fears, and behaviors—are like weather.

Weather arises within, and travels across, the sky. From scattered clouds to violent tornadoes and everything in between. Weather is always coming and going, moving and changing.

Weather moves through the sky, but it never damages the sky. The sky isn't afraid of weather. It doesn't have a preference for some weather over others. The sky doesn't say, "Light drizzle is okay, but that lightning is crossing the line."

The weather hits hard at times, but it's self-correcting. There is never anything you or I have to do to help the weather change. Weather isn't constant. It's not parked. It's always in flux.

The sky doesn't confuse itself with the weather. It doesn't identify with it or take it personally. London sky isn't proud that it rains so often, and Miami sky doesn't feel shame because its clouds don't produce snow. The sky doesn't have ownership over weather. Weather simply passes through the sky, leaving the sky fundamentally untouched.

You are the sky, and your experience is human weather.

Like rain, sleet, and tornadoes, thought, feeling, and other experience arise within, and travel through, you. Human experience comes and goes on its own. Just like you can't make it stop raining, you can't control your human weather. Trying to "stop crying or I'll give you something to cry about" or trying to think a positive thought or trying to feel confident when you want to disappear almost always makes things worse. It doesn't occur to children to try to change their feelings, and we remark at how resilient they are, how quickly emotion moves through them. It works the same in all of us when we don't interfere.

Just as weather doesn't damage the sky, human weather doesn't damage who-you-are. Your essence is one of health, clarity, and peace. It's not even possible for it to be damaged, or fundamentally altered in any way, by impermanent experience. To who-you-are, all experience is safe and welcome.

That probably isn't how it feels, and it's not what we've been told. It may feel like trauma *did* leave a mark, and you've never been the same since, but I'd like to offer another possible explanation to consider. Don't take my word for it, but ask yourself, "What if this were true?" and see what lands with you.

As you've seen, your mind provides a storyline for everything, filling in blanks, connecting dots, and inferring meaning. Our left-brain interpreter can turn a single event, like abuse or a loss, or a single feeling, like fear or grief, into what comes to look like a meaningful statement about who-you-are. From that single event or feeling, a story is quickly spun about what it means about the kind of person you are. The story is full of assumptions, implications about the experiences you're likely to have in the future, and strategies for staying safe.

Your brain is trying to help you. It interprets the jolting nature of this event as something it needs to help you make sense of, which is very kind of it, except that as we've seen, the "sense" it makes isn't all that accurate. Your brain generalizes strong, confident conclusions from very limited, very biased information. Often these events happen when we're quite young. In those cases, it's the brain of a three- or four-year-old drawing conclusions about our safety that can appear real for a lifetime.

The brain has a strong negativity bias in that it processes, stores, and recalls potentially threatening information faster and more easily than neutral or positive information (Alberini 2010; Cacioppo, Cacioppo, and Gollan 2014). This is adaptive overall, but leads to many incorrect, negatively slanted conclusions along the way.

When those traumatic things happened, the emotions you felt didn't feel like safe human weather that would pass on its own. Who-you-are was still okay. It always is. You were still the blue sky. But everything in your psychology was thrown into a tailspin that would not be easily forgotten. It's as if your mind, trying to protect you, responded to those feelings by saying, "Never again!" It scrambled to make sense of things on your behalf, to give you a solid sense of security, an updated sense of self, and a plan for avoiding this feeling in the future at all costs.

When scary things happened, your human weather began to look different. Your thoughts, feelings, and experiences didn't appear safe. They appeared like something to resist and avoid.

Your thoughts, feelings, and experiences didn't appear in flux or fleeting. It appeared as if your mind could be stuck in fear or desperation or anticipation of what might happen next.

Your thoughts, feelings, and experiences didn't appear impersonal. Your mind related what you felt back to "you," the new, fragile, different "you" since that scary thing happened. Your left-brain interpreter's stories may have become faster and more extreme, and your inclination to take them as truth may have grown as they looked increasingly necessary. You may have felt the effects of those stories physically and emotionally. They take the form of anxiety, depression, or chronic pain.

What if our thoughts, feelings, and experiences were safe, fleeting, and impersonal all along, and we just can't always see that through the compelling stories our narrator tells? No one tells you you're okay, that you're just feeling painful-but-safe human weather moving through. The world tends to treat us as if we're damaged. That's the prevailing paradigm.

Weather patterns, thought patterns, and emotional patterns are fluctuations of energy. Fluctuations of one, single energy taking rotating, impermanent form.

Rain, sleet, wind. Sadness, fear, anger.

Same, same, same. And behind them all is a sky that welcomes them in, a sun that's always shining, whether or not we see it through the weather.

This is one of those moments when a mind might be listing exceptions, telling you why this is too simple to be true, or why this is not the case for you.

Or it may be one of those times when a mind is glossing over what you're reading, not pausing so you can truly take it in, dismissing this as something you already sort of know.

This weather metaphor is as accurate as they come. Sit with the enormity of it. Yes, I am saying that it's impossible for you, the real who-you-are, to be damaged, or even permanently impacted, by moving-through experience. Tell your mind that you hear its objections, but still, what if this is true?

The worst that can happen is that you can *feel* damaged due to the physical and emotional human weather you experience. You can *think* you've been damaged. Your mind might then carry around that "damage" in the form of repetitive thoughts, anxiety, or physical health issues that look like clear-cut proof of your damage. But that's not damage, it's thought, and thought is always changing on its own. It's not at all the same thing.

It's habitual, inaccurate, temporary, safe, "I've been damaged" thoughts and feelings that are not you, and they're not yours. They are simply moving through your clear blue sky.

* * *

What if who-you-are remains untouched by any thought, feeling, or circumstance you've ever experienced?

What would that mean for your resilience?

Just Another Thought

If we only experience thought, not what's happening in the world around us, how is it that we have such similar responses to things? Everyone would be devastated at the death of a loved one or elated at winning the lottery, wouldn't they?

Visit my website, https://www.dramy johnson.com/justathought, to hear me speak to this question.

8. Impersonal

Imagine light pouring through a kaleidoscope.

Formless light hits the kaleidoscope and takes form in the shape of colorful patterns.

We no longer call those colors and shapes "light," although of course they still are. We forget the formless essence and focus on the visible shape our senses can grab on to, which our mind can happily classify and label. "Light" is now "a purple, red, and blue triangle pattern."

Minds love to know things. So concrete, visible, and specific are right up their alley.

When you turn the kaleidoscope dial a smidge to the right, the purple, red, and blue triangles turn into a spiderweb pattern with shades of yellow and orange. The formless essence hasn't changed— it's still light—but it manifests into different form. One more click to the right and the yellow and orange spiderweb pattern is now a series of blue and green circles and ovals.

Our human experience works in a similar way. Our essence is formless energy, like the light pouring through a kaleidoscope. Our formless essence is constantly turning into temporary form and then returning to formlessness. Energy takes shape as a human body, for example, a distinct "something," which eventually breaks down and turns back into "nothing." Whether energy is taking temporary form as a cloud, or a ball of hail, or as a thought, feeling, teardrop, or laugh, it's the same universal process. It's all a single formless essence taking temporary form.

Just like we stop calling the colorful patterns in a kaleidoscope "light" when they take on more specific, visible, nameable forms, we do the same when it comes to our human experience. We lose sight of the energy that is our true essence. Of course we do; it's invisible. We trade it for the dynamic, seemingly solid experience our mind can grasp and imbue with meaning.

We use adjectives, labels, and identifiers and pretend they are the truth of it. You're an extraverted person who gets antsy. You have an addictive personality. You used to be a risk-taker but now you're cautious. The parade of always-changing thoughts, feelings, identities, and opinions begins to look more solid and real as a mind flavors them with backstory and significance. A mind tries to cement them into place and write our names on them in permanent marker, connecting them to bundles of thoughts about the concept called "me."

Our mind wants a rational story, so it's constantly connecting dots to create coherence that appears certain and safe. To our mind, we feel anxiety *due to* that upcoming meeting, *because of* how the last meeting went, and because of *what it will mean* about us if this one doesn't go well. But those external events are not the direct cause of a thought or feeling. Events in the world can't create a thought or feeling within us. It doesn't work that way.

Minds tell stories that feel logical and likely, but they are full of bias. A mind will see Frank act rudely to a waiter and expect rude behavior from Frank all the time, regardless of how many nice things Frank does. Your mind will discount what's invisible—things like Frank's state of mind or his mood—and base its judgment on what's concrete and visible: what Frank said or did in a single moment in time. This is called the fundamental attribution error (Ross 1977). Our judgments are exceedingly contaminated, but our mind passes them off as if they were clear and obvious truth.

Our machine-mind takes in sensory information and instantly weaves it into a tale that connects dots and tells stories faster than a kaleidoscope transforms light into patterns.

The stories feel personal because the content is about you. But the story is just the story. The story is just what a left-brain interpreter does. It's a story, not the truth. It's a universal process. Beyond the surface-level content, characters, and storyline, when we really look, there's nothing personal about it.

As we listen closely to the mind's portrayal of things, we forget that form is always changing, that thoughts and feelings are always coming and going, always ebbing and flowing. The formless gets forgotten, while the form gets all the attention.

In the case of our human experience, the apparatus through which energy flows is not a kaleidoscope. It's a brain. Our brain is a physical apparatus full of "stuff" that the invisible, formless energy of life can bump into. Rather than light bumping into colored glass and coming out as shapes and colors, energy bumps into well-worn neuropathways that represent old thoughts, insecurities, or memories the mind views as important.

That energy hits your brain and is shot off in one direction or another. Your mind loves habits and efficiency, so it's often shot off in the same direction it was shot off in yesterday.

Or, it's shot off in the direction that's very emotional, or the one your brain remembered because it thought it was more likely to keep you safe. Every day on her way to work, Lucy's mind turned formless energy into lay-low-don't-make-a-mistake thought form. Hannah's mind habitually funneled formless energy into a be-better-eat-starve cycle.

These directions—these habitual thoughts—aren't as meaningful or stable as they seem. They are just part of the constant costume changes formless energy goes through to give us an array of experiences.

Looking back to our weather metaphor, consider that you aren't responsible for your human experience any more than you're responsible for the weather. Formless energy is constantly taking temporary form. You experience the form, and then it changes. But this is what we say:

"I feel guilty for even thinking this way."

"What kind of person would do such a thing? Why can't I get my act together?"

"It's been six months. I should be over this by now."

"I'm sorry for being so emotional."

Those statements are like saying:

"I feel guilty that the sun is out again."

"What kind of person would have this many cloudy days? Why can't I get my act together?"

"It's been three hours. The snow should be melted by now."

"I'm sorry it's raining."

You don't purposely create your thoughts and feelings. I mean, if I ask you to imagine the Great Wall of China right now, you can conjure up an image. But you don't go through day-to-day life actively conjuring stuff up. Experience is created *through* you, not *by* you.

If you aren't in charge of the experience that moves through you and you don't intentionally create your thoughts or feelings, why in the world would you judge yourself for them? It is like blaming yourself for the weather pattern that's moving through your town.

What, because it's moving past *your* town, it's *yours?* It says something about you as a person?

Your thoughts and feelings are no more personal or meaningful than the weather. You've only *thought* they were for a long time. Ever since you've been old enough to think about yourself and your thinking. Ever since you've been old enough to cling to and personalize your moving, changing experience, it's looked as if what you experience is you. It's looked like your psychological experience means something stable about who-you-are at your essence.

It is not, and it does not.

That was nothing but a simple misunderstanding.

When we don't cling to the temporary form, our experience appears to change more quickly and naturally. It becomes less serious and more fun, like flipping through a kaleidoscope for the sake of watching light change form.

We get to live through a wide array of colorful thoughts, feelings, stories, and interpretations as part of our human experience and not lose sight of the fact that who-we-are is the wise, creative, formless energy that is the source of it all.

* * *

Do you see how personally you take thought and feeling at times? Can you imagine the freedom in seeing that they're not personal?

9. Jelly

I'm sitting on the brown leather couch in my office, shaggy knit slippers on my feet, feet propped on the swivel chair that sits at my desk, laptop on my lap. Our nine-week-old puppy, Jelly, is next to me, chasing letters as they appear on the screen.

Her ears go back, tiny tongue comes out. She *loses her mind* when she sees movement. My fingers dancing across the keyboard is a party for Jelly, and a blinking cursor? Forget about it. I try to get in a sentence or two before moving my right arm out like a windshield wiper, wiping Jelly to the back of the couch.

She lives for this. She's a puppy, and this is what puppies do. They chew and bite and chase and play and growl and run and sleep and then do it all over again.

This adorable little creature isn't trying to delete this book. She's not trying to draw blood on the kids' ankles as her puppy teeth come in, ruin our hardwood floors, or pee on the rug to torture us.

She's not cruel. She's not out to get us. She's not broken. She's a puppy, doing what a puppy does.

We've come to expect our mind to behave the way we want it to rather than pausing to understand how minds naturally operate.

It would be like bringing Jelly home for the first time and after a few hours saying, "This one's too hyper. Her bark is too squeaky. She doesn't work the way we imagined."

It'd be like us complaining to our friends, "Ours is always chewing things. There's no way other puppies chew this much. She has to be outside the normal range."

Or taking her to the vet, saying, "This one's broken. Can you fix her? Can she be rewired? Can we willpower the puppy out of her?" Or asking the vet, "Why is she doing this to us? What did we do to deserve this?"

This is what we've done to our mind. While it's just doing what minds do, we've taken it personally and much too seriously. We've tried to rewire and retrain it. We've tried to ignore it into silence and shame it into submission.

We've called it broken, out to get us, too much, too loud, too active, too negative, too...and then we've wondered why we feel worse. We've wondered why our self-flagellation doesn't lead to change.

I've done these things too. We all do, until we wake up to what minds do.

What we haven't often done is seek to understand why a mind does the things it does. Why is it so repetitive and loud? Why does it tell inaccurate stories and suggest things that aren't good for us?

It turns out, there is a good explanation for your mind's tricks. Everything it does is for your protection and survival—or so it thinks anyway. It's a very smart machine that isn't always wise, but it loves you. It's as innocent and well-meaning as our adorable little Jelly.

It's as loyal as man's best friend.

* * *

What if you saw the output of your mind with the same innocence and understanding you'd have for a puppy?

10. Nothing You Think Is the Truth

Eight kids from the neighborhood are playing telephone in my backyard. The phrase is "Koala bears are cute, and panda bears are cuddly."

Willow whispers it to Sergio, who repeats it to Lilly, who passes it along to Lucas. Lucas tells Allie, who tells Maria, who tells Miller. By the time Miller whispers the phrase to Liam, it comes out as "Koalas are cute when they cuddle with panda bears."

I imagine this is how our thinking always works.

By the time formless energy is filtered through the hallways and tunnels of the survival-focused, me-me-me-loving physical appliance known as the brain, what gets spit out is an idiosyncratic manifestation of formless energy, similar to the way the shapes and colors spit out of a kaleidoscope are mere representations of the light that went in.

No thought is the truth.

Of course, the things we think appear to be true. You think, *He's mad at me,* and minutes later he tells you he is. You think, *That tree is a maple,* and two books, six friends, and the internet agree.

But I'm saying something different. I'm saying that no *thought* is The Truth with a capital *T.* By definition and by design, the content of human thought is subjective and unavoidably tainted. If it were a science experiment, it would be contaminated by the mind through which it passed.

If someone thought it, it's a thought, not The Truth.

If someone thought it, *someone* thought it. That means *someone else* would think it differently. Who's right? Who, of nearly eight billion people on earth, thinks The True thought?

As we've explored already, language is a series of agreed-upon representations that are more like the menu than the food. We can all point to the picture of the spicy tuna roll, but we'll each have a very different experience of eating it. Your six friends might agree that the tree is a maple, not an oak, pine, or birch, or that he is mad, not happy, sad, or bored. But even when we agree with each other at the level of our conceptualized language, each of us is living in our own moment-to-moment, thought-created experience. Our thought-created experience is never a perfect match with anyone else's, or with our own experience in another moment.

Experience comes to life within us in vivid color with emotion and detail, backstory, context, and a ton of supporting evidence generated by our mind. Of course we mistake it for The Truth. It's the reality in which we live. We're immersed in it like the fish in water saying, "What's water?"

Years ago, when my husband and I were a few months into our relationship, there was a day that now lives in infamy between us as "the Village Deli incident."

We were at our favorite breakfast spot, Village Deli, discussing our upcoming trip. We were about to travel to his hometown where I would meet his family for the first time.

Things were going great in our relationship, and I was excited to meet his family. But that morning, I was feeling insecure. It all felt too real, like things were moving too quickly, and I freaked out. I said I didn't know, maybe I wasn't ready for this, maybe we weren't as good together as I had thought. In a matter of minutes, I had gone from thinking about which jeans to pack to feeling an old, familiar inclination to sabotage this nice relationship with this loving, available man. We walked into Village Deli excited and in love and walked out forty minutes later baffled and disoriented. Nothing had changed but my mind.

This was not a new relationship pattern for me, but my sweet husband has the kindest heart and none of this kind of baggage. I hated myself for putting him through this. He had to work a twelve-hour shift that day and was going to come over after work so we could finish our discussion.

In that half day, I experienced an enormous river of thoughts and feelings, most of which came to life as real and true as they flowed through. I felt confused, broken, and incapable of being in a healthy relationship, followed by little glimmers of thought that said, *Maybe that's the old story. Maybe you aren't as broken as you feel.*

There were moments when the only responsible thing to do was to take a vow of lifelong isolation, saving nice guys like my husband from my psychological issues. Those moments were followed by memories of myself as a loving partner, as capable as anyone of being in a stable relationship.

I'd be flooded with love and gratitude for him, followed by memories of things he had said or done that, from my current state of mind, looked like red flags. My mind ping-ponged from one extreme to the other for hours, while something in me knew to stay out of the ping-ponging as much as possible. I didn't interfere. I didn't try to figure it out or make sense of it. I surrendered to it all and knew that some greater wisdom was in charge.

My overactive mind eventually exhausted itself and slowed down. Shortly before part two of our breakfast discussion, the conflicting thoughts and extreme feelings moved out the way, the same way clouds part and the sky opens up after a big storm. I looked back at the past twelve hours like I was looking back on a strange dream. It's not that my worries and questions were resolved. I didn't get answers to the questions my mind was asking, but I saw that I didn't need them. I would see my way through those concerns in real time, if they needed to be seen through. Nothing was resolved, but it looked like nothing needed to be, at least not that day.

I felt lost in the storm while it moved through, but once it had passed, I deeply knew that the storm was a storm—not reality—and it had clouded my vision. I could be in a stable relationship. That wasn't what my mind was used to telling me, but when my mind fell quiet, I knew it to be the truth. I came out of that experience knowing that storms would roll through, but that they would also pass. When they did, things would look different.

How did I know to trust my post-storm thoughts and feelings more than the stormy ones? All I knew was that they felt completely different. With each extreme thought throughout the day, my mind jumped on board like a lawyer presenting evidence and arguing her case. *If he was the one for you, you wouldn't be crying in your pancakes!* My mind brought in exhibits and evidence and even tried to call in witnesses in the form of friends and exes who had seen me through this before. For all the evidence that was presented, nothing felt settled. But what was revealed when my mind fell quiet felt deeply settled. Not full of confidence or a knowing that we'd eventually have a happy marriage. Just that we *could*. What I knew for sure was that I didn't need to worry about all of this now.

The clearing that showed up at the end of that day felt like returning home. Our psychology can be dramatic, but this was the absence of drama. This newfound clarity was still coming to me via thought of course, and no thought is The Truth. But when I stopped looking toward my always-changing mind for clarity, I found that something bigger and less subjective was there all along.

I knew that things might look different at any point, but this clarity was enough for me to recommit for the time being. It was enough to let myself relax into this stable relationship even when my mind said it was boring or too easy. It was enough to meet his family and keep letting life live us, moment-to-moment.

That was nearly seventeen years ago, and we're still letting life live us moment-by-moment. I know to place my attention and trust on the space beyond my busy mind. The more I've looked there, the less my mind has voiced the sort of dramatic concerns it used to.

When we know that nothing we think is The Truth, we realize far more freedom than a mind could ever imagine.

We're free to let experience wash through us without taking it all so seriously. We're free to let formless manifest into impermanent form and then wash away, without needing to identify with it, worry about it, fix it, or try to change it.

We have the freedom to know that we're wearing a helmet of thought, living in our own always-changing reality that will look true as it moves through. Life appears the way thought is creating it, and then thought shifts and it all changes.

Nothing we think is The Truth.

* * *

What if our thoughts are representations rather than truths?

What would this mean for your painful habitual thinking, in particular?

11. Life Lives Us

If no thought is The Truth, and what we experience as reality is always changing, how do we know anything? How do we make it through life?

We are lived.

We're moved through life by the formless energy that is who-we-are. It guides us, bringing experience to life moment-by-moment in real time.

We're lived by the space beyond temporary, fluctuating form, where both everything and nothing exists. That infinite intelligence is pure potential, pregnant with everything, and also completely open and void of any *thing*. It's the space before concepts, ideas, and identities, before all thoughts and feelings.

We're lived by the same intelligence that grows flowers, spins planets, and divides cells to create a baby. We have no responsibility when it comes to life living us. Life is not yours to manage, but don't tell your mind that. Life feels risky and tenuous, like it's our job to get it right, but only because our mind narrates it that way.

On one level, it appears as if we're responsible for saying and doing the right things, we have some degree of free will, and we make choices throughout life that matter. And on another level, you have to wonder: If we aren't in charge of the way formless energy manifests through us, creating what we see as our options and possibilities, to what degree are we truly in charge?

Perhaps it's more that life is living us—actions are taken, thoughts are thought, feelings are felt—and then the narrator tells a story in which we made it all happen. As the main character in your particular game of life, every storyline revolves around you. The game is more exciting when you, as the main character, have agency over what happens next.

We're conditioned to see the free will, I'm-pulling-the-strings side of things. It's the life-is-living-us part that's less familiar (at least to people in Western culture, at this point in history). And the life-is-living-us side of things is the one that's so freeing. Thoughts, feelings, and concepts are form—they *are* creation, so they can't *do* the creating. They are manifestations of the intelligent universal energy that powers all things, not the source of it.

You are lived.

Maybe you aren't getting yourself out of bed in the morning. Your mind might be having a conversation that sounds like, "Is it time to get up already? It's late, you better get moving," but is that conversation *making you* get up and move? Or is that just your mind providing the soundtrack to what's already happening? Have you noticed how sometimes, your mind is saying, "Get moving," when you already have two feet on the ground? Perhaps life is moving you, and your mind is having a conversation about it.

You aren't breathing your lungs or digesting your lunch. Life does that through you.

You aren't plucking your own thoughts and feelings from out of thin air and having them show up in your experience, but your mind is having a conversation in which it feels like you are. We all know what it feels like to have a brand-new idea come "from out of the blue." You've been showering or running or driving and had the solution to a problem just "hit you." But if you really look, isn't that how all experience works? Doesn't everything come from out of nowhere?

When you're wracking your brain for something to make for dinner, you feel your mind churning through options and possibilities. You're aware of effort being devoted to the task. You're aware of thoughts like, *Let me think...what ingredients do we have on hand? What will the kids eat without too much complaint?* You're aware of thoughts like, *Spaghetti? No, we just had that. Mexican? Maybe...let me Google that enchilada recipe I made a few months ago.* You're aware of yourself opening a browser window, entering a search term, and finding something that you appear to choose.

Churning through pros and cons and options and possibilities feels different than when *Let's make enchiladas tonight* seems to hit you from out of the blue on your morning run. But is it really different? Didn't the thought about spaghetti and then the memory of those past enchiladas also come "from out of the blue"? All experience arises within us. Of the infinite forms that formless energy could have taken, it landed on enchiladas. Your brain, with its memories and knowledge, may have contributed to the funneling of formless energy toward the specific form of enchiladas. But you didn't purposely, actively *make* those thoughts or choices happen.

If I had thrown my hands up in that scenario and said, "I give up! I can't make a dinner decision," a decision would still show up. Something would have been eaten, or maybe a meal would have been skipped. Life would live us through that night the way it lives us through every night.

This is the best news ever.

We're lived by something that knows what it's doing, and we get to go along for the ride, interacting and playing and expressing whatever agency and free will we appear to have along the way. There is little we *must* do, but there is infinite possibility in what we *get to* do, think, feel, and experience.

Knowing that life is living you takes so much off your plate. It takes so much off your mind, which makes seeing life beyond your mind's conversations far easier.

Life is a fantastic game to play when you know you're playing a game. When you see that you're lived, there's a safety net built into your experience. Nothing is as serious or up to you as it appears.

Life has your back, even while your mind tells you it doesn't.

* * *

What if life is always living you, independent of the narrator's conversations?

Can you imagine how much time and mental energy might be freed up if you deeply saw this?

12. Feelings

Feelings run our lives.

Nearly everything we do is for the purpose of feeling more of what we like and less of what we don't like.

We seek out things like romantic comedies, mystery novels, and roller coasters for what we feel when we watch, read, or ride them.

When you visit your family, take a vacation, or clean the house, it's because of the feelings you want to feel or those you want to avoid feeling if you were to not do those things. If you dislike your job, partner, or hair color enough, you'll soon find yourself dreaming of different jobs, partners, or hair colors, all because your mind tells you they will deliver different feelings. (Jobs, partners, and hair don't create feelings at all, but your mind doesn't know that.) Approaching what we call good feelings and avoiding what we call bad feelings is behind everything we do.

If our life revolves around feelings, you'd think we'd know what a feeling actually is, and what it's made of and how it works. We use language to label and describe feelings, but deeper than labels and descriptions, what *is* a feeling?

There are many ways to answer that question, but for the sake of our exploration, consider that feelings are fluctuations of energy to which our mind attaches words and stories. Our left-brain interpreter labels and defines the energy dancing through us. So, when we talk about feelings and emotions, we're experiencing two things: the movement of energy plus our mind's commentary on that energy.

Thought and feeling are two sides of the same coin—one formless energy experienced in different forms of psychological experience. Feelings are the felt part of thought.

There's a conversation that's often retold between motivational speaker Tony Robbins and Bruce Springsteen. Bruce apparently told Tony that before a big show, his stomach is in knots, he feels nauseous, and his heart pounds. You might think The Boss has performance anxiety, but he doesn't experience it that way at all. He said when all those physical feelings kick into high gear, he knows he's pumped and ready to put on an amazing show. The energy is fluctuating in ways that a mind could call fear or nerves, but Bruce's mind calls it energized and ready to play.

Feelings are energy moving through us, plus a subjective, biased story about that energy.

When the energy moving through you is low and your mind is thinking about your beloved cat who died, your mind calls the energy sadness. When your mind experiences low energy as stagnant and unchanging, it might call it depression. When your mind embraces low energy, you might say you're feeling peaceful.

When the energy is faster and you're walking into a job interview, your mind might call it nervousness. Feel that same physical energy at the top of a roller coaster and it's exhilaration. The same one energy is the source of everything. How you experience it in any given moment is down to the interpretative story your mind happens to tell. Your mind goes through this interpretation and labeling process in an instant. As we've seen, it's how it makes sense of life and attempts to keep you safe.

Vacillating energy isn't good or bad, comfortable or uncomfortable, in and of itself. It's just energy. The meaning our mind attaches to it is what leads us to like or dislike what we feel.

If fear, for example, were a concrete thing that felt objectively uncomfortable, how would we explain haunted houses and horror films? We pay good money and wait in line for hours to feel afraid. Humans love feeling a wide range of emotions, including terror, sadness, and uncertainty. What we don't love are some of the stories that arise around those energy fluctuations. When our mind says the fear is because of something about to happen *to us,* all bets are off. When the sadness has a me-centered story attached, we push it away.

I once heard a physical pain expert say that what we call physical pain has heat and/or pressure at its core. Meaning, when we look beyond our subjective experience, some combination of heat and/or pressure is present when a person experiences pain. Heat and pressure are physical sensations. They aren't inherently painful, they are just heat and pressure. Our mind calling sensations "pain" and then our resistance of them are what helps create our experience of physical pain.

In *the pain = physical sensations + story* and *feelings = energy + story* equations, it's largely the negatively biased, left-brain story that hurts. Isn't it amazing to know that no story is The Truth?

Feelings are constantly changing, as the root of the word "emotion," "in motion," suggests. But it doesn't always seem like our feelings change quickly in part because the way our mind labels fluctuating energy can be habitual and conditioned. When we don't know how our experience works, we take our habitual interpretations as truth, and we innocently create and recreate particular feelings, leading us to believe that feelings linger or need intervention in order to change.

Several years ago, I was preparing to lead a live workshop, and I went to the venue to check on some logistics. I experienced panic attacks for a long time, but at this particular point, I hadn't felt anything I would consider anxiety or panic for at least six or seven years.

At the venue, I began feeling some strange sensations. I remember watching my mind try to interpret them. Was I overly tired? How much sleep did I get the night before?

Did I forget to eat lunch? Was I nervous about something going wrong at the event? Was I coming down with something?

My mind went through a long list of possible interpretations as I felt energy rising and buzzing through me. As the energy rose, my mind sped up its reason hunt. As my mind sped up its reason hunt, the energy rose even more. As the energy fell, my mind slowed down. As my mind slowed down, the energy settled even more.

And then it hit me. I had a deep knowing that what I was experiencing was the sort of thing that would have become a panic attack in the past. The rising, buzzing energy was the same energy I used to feel all the time. My mind used to meet that energy with oh-no-not-again-I-can't-calm-down-make-it-stop. Those interpretations kept me focused on the energy. Staring at the rising energy would give me the experience of it rising and buzzing even more. In my mind's eye, on that day, I clearly saw how a harmless, meaningless shift in energy, plus a scary mind-made story, led to years of panic attacks.

On that particular day, I had a completely different experience of rising, buzzing energy. My mind was calm and curious. It wanted reasons and answers, don't get me wrong, but there was no fear or urgency. With some space, I observed energy fluctuating and a mind searching.

Feelings are not states that exist outside of thought. Fear, insecurity, shame, craving, and excitement don't course through your body—energy does, and then your mind slaps a label on it and determines what you experience.

When you see that the label is not as real or meaningful as it appears, that it's only a mind doing what minds do, feelings don't feel quite the same.

* * *

Can you imagine how every aspect of your life would be different if you were not afraid of any feeling?

Just Another Thought

Don't anxiety, fear, and insecurity give us information about which choices to make? Don't they motivate us into action?

Visit my website, https://www.dramy johnson.com/justathought, to hear me speak to this question.

13. Discomfort

Discomfort is life trying to wake us up. Discomfort is a brilliant alarm system, showing us that we're identified with a teeny, tiny thought-created fraction of who-we-are.

It shows us that we're caught up in a fleeting wave of energy. It shows us that psychological experience is being innocently mistaken for something solid, personal, and true.

Thankfully, Lucy suffered. The tension created when she believed imaginary pictures and stories of making a mistake hurt so much that it got her attention. The discomfort eventually broke her open to an infinitely bigger, freer experience.

Thankfully, Hannah suffered. Her eating disorder was not something to medicate away, fix, or cope with. It was a wake-up call, urging her to not take her mind-created limitations as truth. Her discomfort ultimately woke her up to who-she-is beyond labels and traits.

Thankfully, I suffered. Our discomfort allows us to remember a bigger truth about who-we-are that extends far beyond the mind strategies and old stories we're identified with.

When we get lost in our mind's narrative and temporarily forget who-we-are, which we so often do, we feel discomfort. Discomfort is the built-in alarm that alerts us to our misidentification.

Discomfort is always whispering, "You're bigger and freer than you currently see." It whispers, and when we don't listen, it screams. Suffering is always life trying to wake us up.

Consider the end of an important relationship. That relationship was important in your life as a human being, of course. You'll grieve it psychologically, and you'll pick up the pieces circumstantially. But it never had anything to do with who-you-are.

It didn't provide anything that the whole of you needed. The whole of you needs nothing. Your mind will tell you what this relationship gave you, and it will list everything the end of the relationship is taking away. But that's only a mind's negativity bias, your mind trying to know everything so it can predict your future.

There is nothing that can be taken away that is necessary for your peace of mind, your happiness, or your ability to give and experience love. Those are who-you-are beyond your mind's story about what you need.

When your mind told you that you needed this relationship, you suffered. As you should. Your suffering was there to show you that you were believing a lie.

It's the same with the business that folded, the weight you never lost, the chances you never took. You didn't need those things to be happy, whole, or good enough, and the absence of them can't ultimately hurt you. When your mind tells you otherwise, you feel that lie in the form of discomfort. Thankfully, you suffer.

It hurts when we are a fraction of ourselves. It hurts being a pure-gold Buddha covered in dirt. It hurts when your child believes what the school bully called him or what his inner narrator says about him. The pain is an alarm clock trying to wake us up.

Are you letting the alarm wake you up, or are you trying to smash the alarm clock? Are you trying to kill the messenger?

I tried to kill the messenger with food and accomplishment safety nets for years. We kill the messenger when we distract or medicate or numb or avoid or try to outrun discomfort without pausing to see what it's showing us. The messenger is trying to point us home, but we don't want to hear what it has to say. We try to mute it instead. We continually hit the snooze button and wonder why it's getting louder.

A colleague once told me about a Muslim man named Ahmed he had been helping with anxiety. Ahmed was no stranger to discomfort, having frequent panic attacks with a lot of low-level anxiety in between. My colleague had multiple conversations with Ahmed about the things we're exploring in this book, but nothing seemed to be landing. "We have some very deep conversations, but I just don't think it's clicking yet," my colleague told me. Ahmed intellectually understood that his experience was safe and impersonal, but he was still fearing and resisting it.

There is a beautiful tradition in Islam called *adhan*. Several times throughout the day, Muslims are called to prayer through bells, chimes, or announcements piped through loudspeakers on the street. Several times each day, they are called to stop what they are doing to pray, to look past their mind's narration and toward the quiet within.

In one of their conversations, it occurred to my colleague that this man's anxiety was just like adhan—his discomfort was a "call to prayer" of sorts, showing him that he was caught up in thought and calling him back toward the peace and calm of who-he-is. His panic attacks weren't a problem to fix. They weren't something to eliminate or avoid. They were a loving alarm, no different from the announcements that rang through his town, calling him to stop and look toward something bigger. His panic attacks were calling him home.

As we relax and spend more time in who-we-are, we notice discomfort more quickly. It takes less of it to get our attention.

When tightness or heaviness, or a feeling of fear, lack, or limitation floats into an already-crowded room, we aren't likely to notice. But when it arises within wide-open, peaceful expansiveness, we notice right away. Something foreign appears. Something that is a miniscule fraction of who-we-are is being focused on and, often, misidentified with.

Of course our mind latches on to something in a field of nothing. When we lose sight of expansiveness and focus only on the story, it hurts. As it should.

* * *

What if all discomfort is a loving reminder that you're caught up in your limiting, changing experience?

14. Colette

"I get *so* anxious when all eyes are on me."

Colette sat on her daughter's white four-poster bed. Although her head and shoulders filled most of my computer screen, a gold-framed picture of the Eiffel Tower peeked out from behind her right ear. The room looked like it smelled of baby powder. It reminded me of my daughter's room.

"It's horrible," she said in her Irish accent. "I hate having attention on me. Absolutely hate it. I know it's old thinking, you know? But the physical symptoms do me in. I get flush, like I'm about to pass out, and my heart starts racing."

Even as Colette was talking about the anxiety that keeps her life smaller than she wants it to be, she had a twinkle in her eye, and her mouth was forming a tiny speck of a smile. It's like the real Colette is peeking out from behind this painful, repetitive story, saying, "I'm here, I'm still here! *She* may feel debilitating anxiety, but *I'm* here, and I'm okay!"

"Maybe this is me going into the past too much," she said, "but I know exactly when it started. Do you want to hear?"

Colette grew up in a large family in the middle of what she calls "Holy Catholic Ireland." When she was fourteen years old, her mother was diagnosed with multiple sclerosis. Colette describes how, with her mum's diagnosis, she went from living in the moment, no cares in the world, to instantly having something to worry about.

Colette's father was the town's banker. Everyone in their small Irish town knew each other. Within months of Colette's mum's diagnosis, her father left Colette's ill mum, Colette, and her three brothers and one sister to be with another woman from town. The woman left her husband to be with Colette's dad.

Colette remembers her mum saying to her one day, "You know, the whole town is talking about us." Colette's entire body burned with shame for her mother whose husband had just left her, unwell, with five children. And it burned with shame for herself. Colette remembers wanting to disappear so no one could talk about her or her family ever again.

A few months after her dad left, Colette stopped wanting to audition for the school plays she used to love, and she stopped trying out for sports teams. She was flooded with worry and the all-consuming feeling that everyone was judging her, so it felt easier to leave those activities behind.

Three decades later, although Colette no longer lives in Ireland, although she's now the mum to four children of her own, and although there is no gossip or scandal in her life today, the remnants of that time linger. When a parent from her kids' school yells hello to her from across a crowded supermarket, Colette feels anxiety and an overwhelming urge to hide.

That's how smart—but not always wise—the machine in your head is. The human brain evolved for prediction, not accuracy (Barrett 2020). Colette's brain remembers the shame and perceived ostracism it felt years ago and predicts more of the same today, even though nothing of the sort is happening.

Thirty years ago, a thought floated through Colette's consciousness the way a cloud floats through the sky: everyone's talking about us. That thought-cloud had an energy to it. Colette calls the energy shame or embarrassment. The labels change a bit from person to person or moment to moment, but they're just the labels a mind uses to try to categorize and make sense of passing-by energy.

The shame and the thought that the whole town was judging her family were so threatening to fourteen-year-old Colette's identity that her mind remembered them. It remembered them far too well, actually. Thirty years later, Colette's super-smart computer mind is still trying to protect her with the ideas it made up so long ago.

It's a little like the game memory we played as children. Do you remember memory?

There was a stack of cards, each with a picture—a red wagon, a yellow tulip, a doghouse, a wheelbarrow. Each picture card had one exact match, so the game contained two red wagons, two yellow tulips... You'd shuffle the cards and lay them facedown, then choose one card. You'd look at your card—let's say it was the doghouse—and then turn over a second card in hopes of finding the matching doghouse. If you didn't get a match, you'd place both cards back where they were, facedown. In time, you began to remember where the pictures were located, so making matches became easier.

This is how our mind works. It detects matches.

Long ago, when the whole-town-is-talking-about-us card was turned over, it appeared so threatening that Colette's mind went into protection mode. And it's been looking for matches ever since.

A neighbor corners Colette out by the mailboxes and wants to hear about her weekend. Match!

Colette is called upon to introduce herself to a group. Match!

A group of moms are talking at Colette's daughter's soccer game, and they call her into the conversation. Match!

Because Colette's mind is so smart and it wants to protect her, it's exceedingly overinclusive with the matches. Her mind doles out false positives left and right. They're *all* false positives.

Can you see how impersonal—almost arbitrary—it is that Colette experiences this the way she does today? It may seem personal because her anxiety comes directly from her life. It comes from *her* mind's response to *her* mum's comment.

But it was one thought in one moment—a thought that never had to occur—that set all of this into motion. If Colette's mum had said, "You know, the whole town is talking about us," and Colette had thought, *Eh, they'll get over it,* would Colette think of herself as "socially anxious" today, three decades later?

If Colette hadn't been in the room when her mom said, "You know, the whole town is talking about us," then what? What if her mum had *thought, You know, the whole town is talking about us,* but had kept that thought to herself?

Of course, we don't know. But when you think of the infinite number of possibilities, the infinite combinations of what Colette may or may not have heard that day, what her mind may or may not have made of what she heard, how her mind may or may not have held on to its conclusions…it makes you wonder just how deeply personal and meaningful Colette's social anxiety habit really is, doesn't it?

* * *

What did you think in a moment in time that has stuck with you and now looks true?

PART II

THAT'S JUST
WHAT MINDS DO

15. Minds Worry

I learned to worry at an early age.

My mom worried a lot, often aloud, and I had no clue that what she was worrying about wasn't real. You don't as a kid.

We were going to run out of money. We'd have to eat canned soup every night. We were going to lose our house. My dad was going to get custody of me and my sister.

It was all completely real in my mind, and I'm sure it was real in her mind too. But none of it was truly real. None of those things happened.

The things we worry about usually *don't* happen because worry isn't about what's happening in the outside world. Worry is our imagination creating dramatic stories and images that we confuse with reality.

Worry is the natural result of evolution. The modern human brain is about two hundred thousand years old, meaning, it evolved to survive in the environment humans lived in two hundred thousand years ago when survival was tenuous, at best. There were physical threats like famine, predators, and dangerous weather that required nearly nonstop present-moment focus. When a person felt fear two hundred thousand years ago, it was an adaptive response, alerting them to an immediate physical threat. There was a clear and obvious protective action to take—when they took the action, the fear subsided. Scientists call this an immediate-return environment, one in which you get an immediate return on your actions (Martin 1999). Early humans followed their natural instincts in the moment and were immediately rewarded with surviving into the next moment.

Although our brains haven't changed much in the past two hundred thousand years, the world we live in has. We now live in what evolutionary scientists call a delayed-return environment (Leary and Cottrell 1999). There are very few threats to our survival, and most of our actions, like working for next week's paycheck and grocery shopping for tomorrow's dinner, have a delayed return. They don't result in an immediate payoff, and certainly not a life-or-death one. The return on our effort-investment comes sometime in the future.

Because the environment has changed far faster than our brain has, we have a bit of a mismatch. Your brain is still behaving as if you might starve to death or be eaten by a hyena at any moment even though you have a cupboard full of food and you only see hyenas at the zoo. When your mind screams in fear today, it's almost never in response to true danger. And because there's no immediate action to take, the fear doesn't arise and then quickly dissipate like it did in an immediate-return environment. You can't fix a problem that only exists in your imagination, so there's little resolution. With nothing in front of you to immediately protect yourself from, your mind interprets the fear in other ways, by imagining what *might* go wrong. As we've seen thus far, when your mind finds itself wondering what might go wrong, it has no problem filling in the blanks to answer its own question. Its answers aren't accurate, but minds hate uncertainty, so they'll provide possibilities, accurate or not. The evolutionarily adaptive, lifesaving feeling of fear that kept our ancestors alive in an immediate-return environment becomes chronic anxiety and worry about things that aren't real in today's relatively safe world.

Worry feels like it's about what's actually happening to us because our minds tell stories that interact with the sensory information we take in. Let's say my mom caught a glimpse of her account balance on a bank statement one day. The number is an objective thing from the outside world that her mind took in. But literally everything her mind did from that moment forward was a creative process designed to provide certainty and meaning. In an instant, her mind may have calculated our living expenses adding up, or she may have seen the bank number dwindling to nothing and never growing. With zero dollars in the bank (in her imagination only), her mind may have creatively filled in the next steps, such as having no money for food or clothes or losing our home. Because minds love to create meaning and make everything personal, hers no doubt threw in predictions about what that single number meant about our future.

We go along for the ride as our mind spins tales full of detail and emotion. Before you know it, my mom is seeing us living under a bridge, eating canned soup in clothes that don't fit, with no sense that this is pure imagination. It looks like an inevitable reality.

From the state of mind she was in, and because she innocently believed that heavy, fearful feelings were showing her true facts rather than imagination-created fiction, her worries seemed likely to come to pass.

Minds create our reality and say, "I didn't do it." They pull in what they see as proof and say, "That number is real! Look, it's right there on the bank statement!" In a fearful state of mind, our worries look like obvious, likely truth.

If what you imagine actually happens in the world—if my mom and sister and I had lost our house and eaten soup every night—it wouldn't have been because my mom's mind knew. Life unfolds moment by moment—there is no future. There is only a mind, right now, creating stories and images and projecting them outward into the world "out there," into the "future."

"Out there" and "future" aren't real things. They are mind-created concepts. They are thoughts.

I became a world-class worrier by the time I was about six years old. For years, I imagined my mom dying in a car accident. Every time she left us with a babysitter at night, I was convinced that she wasn't coming back. I'd force myself to stay awake until I heard the garage door open and saw her headlights shining into my bedroom window.

I worried about how everyone around me felt. I worried about my pets and my friends and my grades. I worried about my health. Kids my age get brain tumors, right?

My mind went to these places so often that it became white noise, like the train that ran past my house that I never heard. Although I didn't always hear my worry as conscious thoughts, I felt it. I felt it in the form of nervous twitches, nausea and headaches, nightmares, and insomnia.

If I had known how feelings work, I might have recognized those feelings as an indication that I was confusing my imaginary mental creations with truth. But I didn't know how feelings work, so the physical and emotional anxiety looked like more cause for worry. The worse I felt, the more it looked like the things I was worrying about were true and likely to happen, things to take very seriously.

If my mom had known better, she might have recognized her feelings as indications that she wasn't seeing clearly too. But she didn't know, and the truth is the exact opposite of how it feels. It's the opposite of what we're told.

Worry masks common sense and makes everything look more complicated and confusing than it actually is. I often hear from people who believe worry is helpful. "I know I worry more than I need to," they say, "but some worry is helpful, right? It prepares me to solve real problems."

No.

Everything a mind does is *its attempt* to help you survive. The brain's negativity bias and constant predictions were adaptive for the survival of a species in the big picture. But worry is not helpful in and of itself, and it's not helpful today. Worry doesn't prepare you to solve problems because the problems you're worrying about aren't real. And worry is not protective. Just the opposite, it fills your mind with scary scenarios that grab your attention so you're less able to access creativity and common sense. Worry is an alarm showing us that we're caught up in thought.

Preparing can be helpful, but worry is not. Minds worry simply because brains have evolved to.

* * *

What if the things your mind worries about have nothing to do with reality?

16. Minds Compare

After the publication of my book *The Little Book of Big Change: The No-Willpower Approach to Breaking Any Habit,* I created an online school called The Little School of Big Change to help people from all over the world find freedom from unwanted habits and anxiety. All new students start by going through a six-week course before graduating into our graduate community.

I've been running The Little School of Big Change since 2017, and although thousands of people from nearly fifty countries with a wide range of habits and anxieties have been through the school, much of what happens in those six weeks is astoundingly predictable. It's an amazing illustration of what all minds do.

Most people begin the program hopeful, with a bit of healthy skepticism. They know they're embarking on a journey that's different from everything they've tried, but still, they've almost always tried many other things that haven't given them the results they want.

In the first couple of weeks, the students are mostly open and curious. They are considering things they've likely never considered, like who-they-are beyond their inner narrator and that habits and anxieties aren't problems, but solutions pointing them back to what's true. Early on, we discuss how freedom doesn't come from the mind, it's already there, beyond the mind. They begin to pay far less attention to their coming and going thoughts and feelings than they're used to. Students are beginning to see what minds do, and many minds are beginning to fall quiet, even if only for brief moments.

By the end of week two, some students are already experiencing huge shifts in the habits and anxiety that brought them into the school. Others aren't seeing much change in their longstanding issues yet, but they have the sense that something is different. The way they see themselves and their experience is subtly shifting.

There is always a portion of people who haven't experienced much insight yet. Some are inspired by what they are seeing in their classmates, others are a little concerned that they are falling behind their classmates. Overall, most students are taking things in stride. It's only week two, after all.

By week three, minds get a little more serious about "progress."

I don't know what it is about week three. Maybe a mind is okay with about two weeks of hopeful uncertainty before it begins demanding answers. Maybe it's because we're approaching the halfway point in the course and minds decide that their inhabitants should have achieved some mind-made level of change by that point. Maybe minds can now imagine the finish line, so they get busy making fear-based predictions about how things will end up for them.

I'm not sure what it is, but it happens every time. Around week three, minds start comparing themselves to others in more extreme ways than ever. Comparisons, future forecasts, and expectations come out in full force.

"I feel like things are starting to click, but my insights aren't anything like so-and-so's."

"I don't feel the way I thought I would. Am I doing something wrong?"

"Yay me, I'm finally getting it!"

"Everyone else seems to be further ahead than me."

This is what minds do.

Minds think their survival, which is really *your* survival, depends on them knowing all they can about you and your weaknesses so they can save you from future failure. One of their favorite tools for knowing the future is comparison.

Comparison is how the mind secures its position as "safe" and "enough." To a mind, you're safe only when you know what's coming. And you're "good enough" only when you stack up favorably against others or against expectations (also created by your mind) for how you should be.

Constant comparison is not only unhelpful, it's not even remotely accurate. Have you noticed how often you come out on top in the comparison game? Not often. The brain's negativity bias inflates what it sees as your relative weaknesses and overlooks the positive. We think our comparisons are giving us accurate information, but they aren't. Our misunderstanding can be incredibly limiting.

For The Little School of Big Change students, the third week comparisons threaten to get in the way because in truth, *all* of these students were doing just fine before their minds shifted to judging and comparing their progress.

The bigger understanding of who-we-are and what minds do was beginning to land for some, and it wasn't yet for others, and that's just how it goes. If things weren't landing with a particular student yet, my coaches and I would work with them to explore things more deeply. That support is often what would help them see what they weren't previously seeing. That's the whole point of the course. It was never going to be the case that everyone would move through perfectly on par with everyone else.

What my students had seen in two weeks meant absolutely nothing about them, their future, or their likelihood of being free of their habits or anxiety. But as soon as a mind starts making up rules for where it *should* be, and as soon as a mind starts comparing you to everyone around you, things go south quickly. "Ahead" and "behind" are concepts created and defined by a mind. When we take them as truth, we become insecure.

And you know how it goes from there, right?

Imagine Becky's mind decides she's behind. Becky came in with the mind-created idea that her breakthrough around her habit would look a particular way, and her experience hasn't been a perfect match to that idea.

Vulnerability and failure look like very real threats to Becky's survival-focused mind. As a way to protect her, her mind starts comforting her with, "Maybe this isn't for you." Her mind creates lists of ways in which she is different from the others, "reassuring" her that she's not likely to have the experience others are having. This gives Becky an apparent explanation for being behind, which her mind loves. If she has to fall behind, at least she knows why.

Eventually Becky's mind says, "Maybe you should back off, put your energy on something else." Becky's mind thinks she's critically close to failure and she'd be wise to quit before that happens. Becky disengages and stops asking for support in order to prevent disappointment. Because Becky stops engaging, it becomes harder to support her and her fear of failure becomes a self-fulfilling prophecy.

There was no problem. Becky's mind made up the rules for success and failure. It made up the entire game.

Other students in Becky's situation might continue to show up and engage, but if the narrative in their head is telling them this probably won't work, that conversation can interfere. It can be difficult to hear anything new when you're wearing a helmet filled with "I don't get it" and "This won't work for me." We see what we expect to see.

On the flip side, even a student who is seeing things deeply and coming out on top in the comparison game can be hurt by comparisons that look true. Their mind can turn their top-of-the-class status into their new identity, complete with its own mind-created expectations. Now, rather than exploring with an open mind, this student's mind tells them they are special, they better secure their place at the top, they have something to lose. All of that gets in the way when it looks real.

Comparisons are a machine-mind trying to nail down "you," making sure you are good enough to survive. They are a machine-mind trying to nail down the future so there are no surprises.

But you and life and are not nail-down-able. You and life are always safe and thriving. We see this when we look beyond the noise of our mind's comparisons.

* * *

In what ways does your mind love to compare you to other people or made-up standards? Can you imagine how your life would be if those comparisons didn't appear personal or true?

17. Minds Problem Solve

Matthew worked in marketing with a tight-knit team of colleagues who were also good friends. He loved his career, especially the way it challenged his creativity and forced him to solve difficult problems. It was a huge bonus that his coworkers were like family. He couldn't imagine a better arrangement.

Then, one day, there was a misunderstanding.

His team was working with a new client on a high-profile project that was getting a lot of publicity. The stakes were high, and everyone was on edge. A marketing piece that Matthew collaborated on was expected to be a big hit. The team loved it, the client loved it, and everyone felt it would get a lot of attention when it went public. But just before the campaign went live, something in the ads didn't sit well with Matthew. He made an executive decision to make a last-minute change.

Matthew's actions fell outside the typical operating procedure, and it upset some members of the firm. Even some of Matthew's team members—his close friends—had a hard time moving past what he had done. Matthew did what he thought was right in the moment, but others saw it as disrespectful to the team as a whole. They thought it jeopardized the project and eroded trust.

The initial misunderstanding paved the way for many more misunderstandings in the following weeks, and Matthew was eventually asked to resign his position. His friendship with his team members was impacted, and things were never the same. Since Matthew resigned, he's been working at a new firm doing less creative work that he doesn't enjoy.

The team broke up three years ago, and Matthew is in a tornado of thinking about it today.

"How could they see things so differently? How could a simple misunderstanding lead to this? How would my life look now if this had never happened?"

"What does it mean that I'm still thinking about this three years later? Do I need to resolve this in order to be at peace?"

Matthew's mind was working in overdrive to solve this problem for him. But do you see how his mind was also *creating* the problem in real time? Yes, something happened three years ago. But 100 percent of his anguish about it today is coming from his identification with the thoughts, memories, and "what if" scenarios his mind is creating *today*.

Matthew's experience of the problem is a reflection of his mind deciding things should be different than they are. After his mind spits out all of this dissatisfaction, it swoops in to try to clean up the mess it created.

That's what minds do. Our experience is created in our mind, moment to moment. Memories are a creative process taking place in the present moment, the only place anything ever takes place. The content of the stories Matthew was caught up in were about an event in the past, but that's just the subjective storyline. The memory is a brand-new, present-moment thought. All experience is created in real time, and all experience is in the process of changing.

In the name of protection and survival, minds look for unsettled business they can resolve on your behalf. When you're lying in bed, unable to sleep, your mind could create any number of happy memories, but it focuses on problems it can solve, as Matthew's mind was doing. It replays misunderstandings and has conversations with people who aren't there. It replays past disagreements and argues your side as if the debate were actually happening. It finds the things with which you are least comfortable and tries to help you feel better about them. Your mind seems to forget that you were just fine a few minutes ago, before it decided to resurrect the past in order to fix it.

A mind can't leave well enough alone because to a mind, there is no well-enough. There is always more—more to do, more to solve, more to fix. More of your identity to solidify, more security to safeguard.

Now, here's where this can get confusing. Because minds love a concrete, black-and-white formula, yours might be hearing me saying there is no value in the memories or thoughts that arise. But that's not necessarily true. Sometimes, as your mind is rehashing an old misunderstanding, you have an insight that leads you to see things in a brand-new way. In that case, perhaps it was helpful that those old memories came up and allowed you to look at them in a fresh, new way.

But the fresh, new way of seeing things didn't come *from* the mind's repetitive rehashing. Your mind didn't think its way to clarity.

Clarity came from *beyond* the monotonous, chatty mind, from the formless space beyond reasons and repetitive stories. It came from the expansive essence that is who-you-are.

One of my favorite quotes, attributed to Einstein, is "The intuitive mind is a sacred gift. The rational mind is its faithful servant. We've created a society that honors the servant and has forgotten the gift." Intuition is a concept that means different things to different people, but to me, intuition is another way of talking about who-you-are. It's that same pure energy that's at the root of everything. It's what arises within us as something we know, independent of logic and left-brain reasons.

Your chasing-its-tail mind doesn't save the day the way it says it does. It's more instigator, blame shirker, and credit stealer, than the savior. If your mind is such a good problem solver, where was it when the problem was playing out in real time? And if it's so smart and full of clarity, why does it have to repeat itself so much?

Matthew reached out to me near the end of his thought-storm. "It's strange," he said. "Even while my mind is back in the events of three years ago, telling me that things must be resolved, I kind of know better.

"I know I'm ruminating, and that it will eventually stop. What I don't understand is why I've spent a sleepless night and most of the next day ruminating about this if I know better.

"It's almost like I think that replaying all angles of the situation will help. Yet, as I say this, I can see that's not true."

I reminded Matthew that his mind was simply chewing on this the way a dog chews on a bone. Dogs chew bones to release energy. It's soothing and stimulating. It's not about reaching some end result; it's just what they're compelled to do.

Minds too. They chew on things and replay them ad nauseam. It's stimulating and lets them feel productive and relevant. It's how they care for you. If they can solve even one problem, or provide even a little bit more certainty, they've made life safer for you.

"It's only strange if you think you're the one doing it," I said to Matthew. "*You* know better, but you aren't the one trying to solve a three-year-old problem that doesn't exist. Your mind is."

Our feelings show us what our mind is up to. The heavy, confused, repetitive feeling of rumination was there to show Matthew that his mind was caught up in thought that appeared objectively true, but wasn't. This was not an objective problem Matthew had to solve. It was a mind creating thoughts, calling those thoughts "problems," and then attempting to solve those thought-problems.

In truth, there was nothing to solve. Thought comes and goes, no solution necessary.

* * *

Can you see how your mind is the source of many of the problems it tries to solve? Notice how it searches for problems to solve on your behalf.

18. Minds Think We're Never Good Enough

Bethany graduated at the top of her Columbia University Law School class. She was editor of the *Columbia Law Review,* and she landed the internship all of her classmates wanted. After graduation, she passed the bar exam on her first try and took a position with a prestigious global firm based in Boston. Given that she routinely billed seventy to eighty hours per week, you might think she loved her work.

She hated it.

The day we met, she confided that she became a lawyer because she thought she'd feel confident as a partner in a law firm. Her mind created an image of her reaching a level of professional and financial success that would lead to unwavering confidence. A level of success that would prove to everyone—but especially to Bethany herself—that she was good enough. She thought that once she'd "made it," her mind would finally rest.

But it didn't work that way. Instead, with each new level of success and prestige, Bethany's mind upped the ante. It moved the finish line.

When moving up the career ladder wasn't providing the confidence her mind promised it would, Bethany began running marathons. Miles and medals didn't do it either, so she added travel. She went on a pilgrimage to India and traveled to Norway to see the northern lights. She chose both trips because they seemed consistent with the Instagram-worthy life she thought would allow her to finally feel settled. They didn't do it either.

Everything Bethany did was an attempt to fill the not-good-enough-yet void her mind kept pointing out. She wasn't enough *now,* and she couldn't relax *yet,* but *someday…*

We've all heard the commencement speeches about doing what you love and following your heart. And we've seen the refrigerator magnets and social media memes about living in the moment. I know it's familiar and kind of cliché, but please hear this. Life on the "someday" hamster wheel will never, ever end with you finally feeling good enough because of some outside thing you've accomplished. It can't. Your mind won't let it.

Your mind will never tell you that you're good enough. Deciding that you're good enough—that now is the perfect time to enjoy life—is just *not* what minds do.

Your mind will never tell you it's safe to slow down or stop or rest. Minds are in the business of doing. They are in the business of more, not less. They are in the business of producing, not being.

You'll never reach "someday" because there is no such thing. "Someday" is a concept, a thought that minds make up. The minute you think you've reached your destination, your mind will begin its search for the next "someday" port of call.

In all minds at various times, it goes something like this:

Your mind talks about "more" and "not enough," and you shift your attention from who-you-are, always whole and at peace, to that conversation about what's missing. Tuned in to that conversation, you feel like you're lacking.

Because you believe you're lacking, your mind jumps in to help as it's been doing since that first scary thing drove you into your head as a little kid. You look to your mind for ideas on how to stay safe and fill the void, not realizing that your mind is creating the illusion of a void to begin with.

Your mind creates ideas and images that promise to fill you with the feelings you want. Bethany's mind created images of being secure within herself as a partner in a law firm. Mine has created similar images of myself with the right business, the right relationship, being the right kind of mother. Our minds are always creating new solutions to the be-good-enough-so-that-you-survive "problem" our mind creates.

Those new solutions and images feel good, but only because your mind has shifted from saying, "You should be better," to imagining a circumstance in which you *are* better. We live in the feeling of our thoughts, and imagining these "someday" destinations feels better than thinking we aren't there yet.

Your mind reassures you that arriving at that destination, wherever it is, will allow you to relax and feel at home in your life. The ticket to entry is usually hard work and sacrifice today. It'll all be worth it, your mind says. The feeling of home you're looking for is always an arm's length away.

You move toward whatever outcome you've set your sights on. You feel excited and hopeful when you're close and defeated when you're not. Bethany did this over and over, with ever-changing goals and outcomes.

The emotional roller coaster you're on is just a reflection of the ebb and flow of thinking, but your mind uses it as further evidence that success feels good and failure feels bad. Bethany's mind told her, "See how good it feels to be on track for that promotion? Keep striving, you're almost there!" But we lose sight of the fact that our mind is constantly redefining success and failure. We will never arrive "there" by working harder or collecting more accolades.

If you don't get the promotion or finish the marathon or whatever the outcome du jour happens to be, you suffer for a while until your mind creates a new "someday" image for you to work toward. The promise of the new goal brings hope so you feel better. If you do accomplish your outcome, your feeling of satisfaction is astonishingly brief. Your mind quickly creates a new "someday" image for you to work toward, and you're back to where you started: not-enough-yet, searching for what's next.***

Neuroscience research shows that of seven core instincts in the human brain (anger, fear, panic and grief, maternal care, pleasure

---

*** We tend to grossly overestimate how long we'll be satisfied after an accomplishment and how long we'll be dissatisfied after a negative outcome. Feelings don't last, but we're slow to remember that when we're predicting our future (Wilson and Gilbert 2003).

and lust, play, and seeking), seeking is the most significant. Most mammals are rewarded with a hit of dopamine for exploring their environment and thinking ahead, or seeking (Panksepp 2004). As we've seen, the brain evolved to look ahead and predict. That doesn't mean we have to fall for the misunderstanding that the next achievement will bring long-term satisfaction. It only points to why our mind is often seeking.

If striving for the next "someday" outcome that promises a life of fulfillment is what minds do, is there any hope in being free of it?

There is a ton of hope, actually. We are free already. We just don't realize it when we forget who-we-are and believe our needy thoughts.

We see that we're already free when we *see* how our mind works. See that it's your mind dangling those carrots out in front of you. *You* don't necessarily care about those things, and they won't deliver what your mind says they will. It's your mind trying to help you in ways that are not particularly helpful.

Be curious about who-you-are beyond the goals and desires and wishes and fantasies. What if you really do have all the confidence and peace of mind you could ever dream of, right this very minute? What if you're only missing it because you're mesmerized by your mind's plans for your improvement?

No amount of accomplishments, success, love, admiration, money, food, alcohol, or material stuff will fill that void because there is no void. They never worked for Bethany, and they won't work for any of us. We're free to enjoy all the accomplishments, success, love, admiration, money, food, alcohol, or material stuff we'd like, but they won't bring lasting confidence or contentment. They are simply things we may or may not enjoy.

By the way, Bethany is no longer a lawyer. Her hamster wheel led to chronic fatigue, anxiety, and bulimia, which led her to spend the past two years deeply exploring who she is and what minds do.

She's now an organic farmer, expecting her first child. She and her husband restore and resell old farmhouses in rural Massachusetts. She hasn't been on an exotic trip in a long time. She's found that camping in her own backyard is more her style.

When she notices her mind talking about "someday," she thanks it for trying to help, but she's no longer inclined to chase those empty promises. Her life continues to improve the more she lets it live through her in ways that feel natural and right today, not someday.

* * *

What might you choose to do if you knew that you are worthy no matter what you do or accomplish?

19.   Minds Dramatize

As much as minds love to solve problems, compare and contrast, pro and con, and create "someday" carrots to dangle in front of us with the promise of lasting fulfillment, perhaps the thing they do most naturally and most often is dramatize.

Ironically, the drama can be hard to notice. Minds have been adding color commentary, backstory, and emotion to their narration for so long that it usually doesn't sound all that dramatic or exaggerated. It looks like the drama is in life, out there, not in our mind. A mind says, "Who, me? I'm just telling it like it is."

My daughter Willow participates in youth theater. Everything about youth theater reminds me of a mind.

The kids don't just speak loudly in their own voice, they practically scream in their stage voice. They overact. Their lines and movements are exaggerated, full of dramatic inflection. They don't just wear makeup, they cake on layers upon layers of stage makeup so they are sure to be seen. They don't just turn the lights up, they are blinded by the biggest, brightest stage lights.

Everything is exaggerated for effect on stage. And in our mind.

I'm not suggesting that it always sounds like *West Side Story* in your head, I'm just saying that your mind is a storyteller by nature. It brings fluctuations of energy and story together with the sensory information you're taking in, resulting in quite a display. It's a brought-to-life, real-as-can-be experience. It's virtual reality that doesn't appear virtual.

Have you noticed how your mind likes to exaggerate?

I recently had an exceptionally jam-packed month. I was wrapping up a six-week The Little School of Big Change course, which is nearly a full-time venture in itself because of the high level of support each student receives. I had three work trips scheduled that month to different corners of the United States, as well as one to the United Kingdom. At home, Willow was on a three nights per week play rehearsal schedule, my son Miller was on a three nights per week soccer schedule that included a weekend tournament, and my husband—who usually handles a majority of the carpooling and dinner cooking—was called in to work beyond his typical part-time hours because one of his coworkers was out on a medical emergency.

There was more going on than I would have wanted. And the truth is, I felt overwhelmed and in over my head many times that month.

The truth is also that I made some friends for life in the UK, we had some amazing family time at the soccer tournament, and my flights were relaxing and full of helpful, kind people. My husband and I figured things out along the way, and even when dinner was a sandwich in the car on the way to play rehearsal, it was all okay. I felt present and full of love and gratitude many times that month.

When other people would say, "How are you doing so much? You must be jetlagged and exhausted," my mind would jump on board, wanting to milk it for all the drama it could.

Oh my gosh, they're right, I'd think. *I have to get better at saying no.*

But sometimes I'd hear my mind say that and realize that I didn't actually feel that way. Even at the very moment my mind was giving a dramatic rendition of my schedule, I'd feel the calm and peace that is who-I-am. A little voice would say, "Nah, it's not so bad."

Sometimes during that month, I was thinking about the month. I was looking at the calendar, taking stock of how much I had done and what was yet to come. And many times during that month, I wasn't.

A month isn't a thing, it's a concept. Life doesn't know which day of the week it is. Life doesn't know which country you woke up in yesterday and where you'll be tomorrow. Life doesn't know how much sleep you got or which kid needs to be where at what time.

Life is always here, now. A mind, on the other hand, loves made-up concepts like month, busy, time, and jetlag. A mind loves tracking those things and weaving them into dramatic stories full of math. There's sleep math, "If I fall asleep now, I'll still get six hours," mile math, "I've traveled twelve thousand miles this week," family math, "The four of us have only eaten dinner together twice this week."

A mind is a talented calculator, and the calculations it spits out are full of seemingly meaningful but made-up implications, like, "It's not good for your family to be separate and on the run this much," and "You must be exhausted sleeping so little and traveling so far."

So, all month, I watched my mind's drama ebb and flow. I watched it create and solve math equations. I watched it perk up when someone showed sympathy for how much I was doing. I watched it want to jump in with, "I know, it's *so* hard!"

I watched it tell me I deserved a break, even when I didn't necessarily feel like I needed one. It wanted to "reward" me with food, time off, and other things that may have been enjoyable in and of themselves, but were clearly my mind clinging to a story of life-is-so-hard-but-this-someday-reward-will-make-it-all-better. Of course we need food and rest, but if these were true physical needs, they'd be satisfied by instinct, not by a busy mind presenting them in terms of rewards and deserving.

I watched my mind from the place *beyond* the drama, beyond concepts and generalized stories. I watched from the still ocean floor as it made waves on the surface. From that place, life isn't dramatic at all. It's simply life unfolding with something new in each and every moment.

My mind still loves exaggeration, but more often than not, I remember that's just what minds do. When it says things like, "I can't believe he said that!" or "Let me tell you about this crazy day

I had!" it can be fun to share those exaggerated stories, but I know they are stories. They no longer look like how things actually are.

We can't control how turned-up the drama dial is in any given moment, but it changes everything to know there is a drama dial.

* * *

What's your mind's favorite way to dramatize?

PART III

Form *and*
Formless

20. On the Line

When I was growing up outside of Detroit, one in three people worked for one of the "big three" auto companies—Ford, General Motors, or Chrysler. Everyone I knew had a parent, aunt or uncle, or neighbor who worked in the industry. Many of them worked "on the line."

They could have cared a lot about what they created. There could have been truck versus car factions, engine versus bumper versus rearview mirror factions, Ford versus GM versus Chrysler factions.

But they intuitively knew that they were far more alike than different, regardless of the product that came off their line. They could relate to each other at the level of process—they go to work in a factory, dealing in raw materials that are turned into vehicles— not at the level of output. They could relate in terms of what it's like to work on the line. The specific object that happened to be spit off the end of the line was neither here nor there.

When it comes to our human experience, looking toward *how we all work* and *what all minds do* changes everything. It orients us in the direction of a stable, universal process rather than temporary, fleeting form.

We have minds that worry and predict and define and create. There are infinite possibilities for what any particular mind does in any particular moment. The output of a mind could be anything, and it's always tainted by memory and fear and habit and conditioning and a gazillion other factors.

At this moment, my mind is worrying about whether this book will make sense to anyone but me. My son's mind is creating an elaborate fantasy of him getting a hole in one on the last hole of the Masters Cup. My husband's mind is predicting how our upcoming visiting with his parents will go. And my daughter's mind is running a crude probability calculation to judge who—me or her dad—is more likely to let her ride her bike to her friend's house three blocks away. Those specifics make up our experiences of life in this very moment. They are personal and very real to each of us, but with one click of a kaleidoscope dial, or in a matter of nanoseconds in real time, each of our minds will be creating something different.

We live in the creative *process* of life, not only in the momentary creation.

All assembly lines produce. That's their job. Engines, bumpers, rearview mirrors. Plastic bottles, chewing gum, machine guns. All human minds produce too. The fact *that* we think is far more universal and more grounding than *what* we happen to be thinking in any given moment. The fact *that* we are always feeling is far more significant than *what* we happen to be feeling in any given moment.

Roll the dice, spin the wheel, turn the kaleidoscope a fraction of a degree, throw some new raw materials on the line, and the output is completely different. But the fact that always-changing output is produced is constant.

I'm not making a case for dismissing the *what* of our human experience. All assembly lines have to produce specific somethings, just like all minds produce specific thoughts. The what—the worries, fantasies, predictions, preferences, hopes, dreams, memories, fears—are what make up our very human experience of life. They aren't to be discounted or dismissed.

But can you see how caught up in the *what* we tend to get and how much suffering that causes? When we're losing sleep over what might happen, or when we're trying to out-think our intrusive thoughts, or when we walk around feeling as if we've been depressed for decades and change is hopeless, all we see is the output—the content of our experience that feels like a rock-solid statement about who we are and how our life is.

When there is a shadow that looks like a monster on our bedroom wall, it behooves us to remember that the "monster" is actually just light taking a temporary form. The form looks terrifying, but the form isn't solid. Looking toward the essence loosens our grip on the form, and when our grip on the monster isn't so tight, it disappears as the light shifts. It's the same with our fears and insecurities. They change and shift, coming in and out of focus, far more quickly than our mind will lead us to believe.

Like assembly lines, minds produce. That's just what they do.

There is so much freedom in knowing that if we don't like what's taking shape through us in any given moment, something different is already coming down the line.

* * *

Can you see how it's not *what* we think and feel, but *that* we think and feel, that allows us to see our experience for what it is in a clearer way?

Just Another Thought

Doesn't looking toward what we all have in common detract from our uniqueness and sense of self?

Visit my website, https://www.dramy johnson.com/justathought, to watch a video of me speaking on this and other topics.

21. Looking Toward What Never Changes

I'm in a 6:00 a.m. hot vinyasa class balanced in tree pose. I'm standing on my left leg with my right foot rooted into my left thigh. My arms are extended like branches overhead.

I scan the room and immediately remember what a horrible idea that is. As soon as my eyes start moving, my body follows. My left leg and torso sway back and forth. I tighten my core and bring myself back into balance.

"Establish a *drishti,* a gazeless gaze toward something in the room that's not moving," the teacher tells the class.

My eyes settle on a grain of white wood molding where the floor and wall meet, about seven feet in front of me. The instant my gaze settles into that spot, my body is steadier.

When we have something stable to look toward, it grounds us. We feel balanced and secure in tree pose and in life.

The understanding of who-we-are and how we work grounds us. It points toward an unmovable foundation—who-you-are at your unchanging essence is peace, love, and wisdom, full of resilience and health that can't be damaged or taken away. That consciousness, the energic essence of all things, is constant. It's like the blue sky that's always there beyond the weather.

This understanding also points toward what is forever moving and changing: everything else.

Our psychological experience—our thoughts, feelings, and behaviors—are not pin-down-able. Like weather passing through, we couldn't hold on to it if we tried. When you stare at something that's moving, you get dizzy. You feel out of balance, unstable, insecure, and afraid.

In life, we're constantly staring at moving experience. We focus on our angry thoughts about the neighbor's tree on our property, that problem at work, the personal shortcomings we think we need to fix, and we get disoriented, stressed, and dizzy. We get knocked off-center.

Rather than trying to focus on always-moving experience, your secure, stable foundation can be your drishti. The consciousness that is who-you-are is an unmovable truth on which you can rest. Place your gazeless gaze there, and it holds you as experience rises and falls through you.

Knowing that you have this healthy essence, that you are formlessness playing a game in form, allows you to explore, take chances, make mistakes, and fully feel everything there is to feel in life. It's like a child who has a secure attachment to safe, loving parents. The child is free to learn by experience because they have a secure foundation to which they can return. They can live more freely because they have a secure home base.

You also have a secure home base to which you can't *not* return. No experience moving through you sticks. Who-you-are is always revealed from beyond it.

My favorite definition of the word "drishti" has two parts. First, a drishti is something that allows us to withdraw our senses from what's moving. Second—and this part takes my breath away every time I hear it—drishti is a form of self-discovery, a way to know ourselves and to discover what's true.

A way to know ourselves. Our true selves.

And a way to discover what's true. What's true is what's unchanging, beyond our ever-changing experience.

* * *

Notice how everything within and around you is always changing. You couldn't hold on to a thought or feeling for too long if you tried. See if, beyond what's always moving, you can sense an awareness that has been "you" your entire life, never changing.

22. Objects and Processes

Are you an object? Or a process?

What about the psychological experiences that dance through you? Are they objects or processes?

The grateful or self-critical thought you had when you looked in the mirror this morning—was it more like an object or a process?

That twinge of excitement, pang of shame, vivid memory, the taste of your morning coffee, the sound of your favorite song playing...

Your personality, identity, physical body, life...

Objects or processes?

The ocean offers so many metaphors for who-we-are and how our human experience works. We aren't *like* nature, we *are* nature. We are the formless energy of all of life that happens to be taking temporary form as a thinking, feeling human rather than as a tree or flower, but other than the temporary form, we aren't different from Mother Nature. As the poet Rumi told us eight hundred years ago, we are the drop *and* the ocean (often mistranslated as, "You are not a drop in the ocean. You are the entire ocean in a drop," which is also pretty good).

There is a fascinating documentary called *The Secret Life of Waves* that illustrates the object versus process distinction. Waves are a temporary manifestation of ocean. They can be small or large, calm or violent, but their form is always temporary. They always crash on shore and turn back into what we perceive of as "ocean," and then they do it all over again. Ocean to wave to ocean to wave (Malone 2011).

When our mind labels something "wave," we experience it as an object. Not because it is, but because our mind wants to solidify as much as possible so we can have certainty and predictability. To our classifying, concretizing mind, "wave" is an object, somewhat distinct from "ocean," another object. But this thing we call a wave isn't a thing at all. What we call a wave is actually a transfer of energy. It's a process.

What if you're a process too?

Minds want to objectify everything, *especially* you. Especially your identity, your personality, your weaknesses, and to a lesser degree, your strengths.

But when we really look, we're actually processes like waves, aren't we? We are energy. Our experience is always in motion, our thoughts and feelings are always-changing energy.

We are processes, not objects. But our mind is a machine that thinks in an all-or-nothing, linear way. It narrates life in a way that has life looking solid, problems appearing hopeless, and a "you" that can be stuck.

We'll never be free of our mind's linear narration, objectifying everything in sight. A mind won't stop doing what it does, but when you have an understanding of what it does and you know who-you-are beyond the mind's narration, you can be free in it.

Seeing that you're a process, not an object, helps you see the fluidity all around.

* * *

How do habits and feeling stuck look different when you see yourself and your experience as a process rather than an object?

23. You Can't Be Stuck

If we humans are always-updating processes that can't be stuck, why do we feel so stuck at times?

We feel stuck in relationships, in careers, in our "progress," however a mind is defining that. We feel emotionally stuck, like we want to cry but can't, or like we want to scream but shouldn't. We feel like we're missing something, like life is passing us by, or like we're living the same day over and over, stuck in our conditioning.

Feelings show us what our mind is doing, so feeling stuck is a reflection of what we're thinking. Our mind is having a conversation that's cyclical and repetitive, full of commentary about how life should be different than it is. Minds replay sticky stories, but we can't *be* stuck. Life is always moving no matter how sticky our thinking feels. Life is moving while our mind repeatedly tells us how stuck we are. That repeated narrative is what we're focused on, so we come to believe we're stuck.

Tina was a student in my online school, The Little School of Big Change, getting support for anxiety. Her mind spun and worried and constantly asked "What if?" as all minds do at times. But Tina's mind was doing these things so much that her family doctor told her she met the diagnostic criteria for generalized anxiety disorder.

When I met her, she was far less concerned with her worries than she was about the fact that she had been given a diagnosis. The minute there was a label for what Tina "had," she instantly felt defined by that label and stuck in the experience of it.

"I can't believe I have a bona fide, diagnosed, mental disorder," she said. Well, when you say it like that and you're conditioned by society to view a diagnosis as a stable, meaningful problem, it does sound serious. But I just can't see it that way. I've had more than one bona fide, diagnosed mental disorder at various times in the past myself, and I work with amazing, wise, healthy people who do as well. Meeting the criteria for a diagnosis like generalized anxiety at some point in your life is about as common—and about as personally meaningful—as having a plantar wart or an ingrown toenail.

A diagnosis is a label that describes a set of experiences. It is a concept that classifies and lumps together some fleeting experiences. That Tina's mind worried and overthought at times, and that it showed up in her body in the form of a racing heart and sped-up breathing, wasn't a problem, even to Tina. She only viewed it as a problem when it crossed the arbitrary and subjective "too much" line (defined by her mind, of course). That's when she felt stuck in it. The seriousness with which Tina's mind was taking her "anxiety disorder," and the extent to which she viewed it as a stable, personally meaningful thing, was the source of her stuckness and the only problem she had.

It's like when you have a cold. If you knew you'd have some cold symptoms for two days, for example, I bet it wouldn't bother you much at all. It's only when your mind chimes in with a story about how long it might last, how bad it might get, and which plans it might interfere with, that you suffer. That's what minds do. They take fleeting experience and turn it into scary, personally relevant abstractions about you and your mind-made future (Edelman 1990).

Tina doesn't *have* anxiety. We *feel* feelings; we don't *have* them. There is no ownership of energy. When Tina's mind tells her she has an anxiety disorder, she can't help but focus on the fluctuations of energy moving through her, looking to them as confirmation of her diagnosis. She feels stuck. Her mind finds lots of evidence for her *having* anxiety, not because an anxiety disorder is sitting there waiting to be found, but because her mind is looking for it. Tina's mind had to generate thoughts about anxiety in order to look for them. It's like playing hide-and-seek with yourself—you're likely to find yourself when you're the hider and the seeker.

Tina's feelings of stuckness were a mind-created experience kept alive by an innocent misunderstanding of how a mind works.

You can't be stuck. When you feel like you are, you're simply zoomed in on a repetitive, sticky, mind-made story. Feeling stuck is a gift reminding you to back up, soften your focus, and let new experience flow through.

* * *

What if it's not possible to be stuck, but we *feel* stuck when our thinking is repetitive and it tells us we're stuck?

PART IV

FREEDOM

of MIND

24. My Mind's Freedom-Seeking Habit

Most of our personal theories about who-we-are and how we need to be in order to have the security and love we desperately want are born in the moment something scary happens.

Something happens that feels threatening or unexpected. Your left-brain-created identity—and sometimes your physical safety—appear to be at risk, and your mind, because it loves you, comes to the rescue. It makes a plan, in an instant, to make sure you'll never feel insecure again.

One of the first scary things I remember happened when I was about nine years old.

My parents were divorced. My mom was in a new relationship, and I thought the guy she was dating was a jerk.

It wasn't just that I didn't like *him*, I didn't like that she dated anyone. I wanted to live with my mom and sister without a man moving in, and I decided it was time to make sure my mom understood how I felt.

In my nine-year-old mind, my request was perfectly reasonable. I thought about how to state my case. I rehearsed my speech in bed at night. My arguments were ironclad. I remember being so proud of myself for approaching this the way a mature adult would.

I imagined myself stating my case and my mom quietly reflecting on what I said. I imagined her saying, "I understand, and you're right, it *is* much better when it's just us three. I will put dating on hold until you grow up. You and your sister are all I need." She would realize how strongly I felt about this, thank me for being so mature, and break up with the jerk that day.

That's not how it went.

My mom told me in no uncertain terms that she'll be making the decisions about her personal life, thank you very much. She'd be calling the shots, and she wanted a partner, so I had better get used to it. That may or may not be what she actually said—it's probably pretty far off—but it's what my mind extracted from our conversation.

I can still see us sitting at the foot of my bed in my purple, unicorn-themed bedroom, having our talk. My baffled, reeling mind drew two conclusions at once.

One, I was powerless. Other people were able to make decisions that seriously impacted my life, and there was nothing I could do about it. And two, my opinions didn't count. I was foolish to think they'd be heard or respected.

To cope with those conclusions that looked like absolute truths, my nine-year-old mind came up with some strategies.

First, nothing was more important than having the freedom to determine how my life went. I would do everything in the little power I had to pave my own path from that moment forward. How this looked in my life was constantly evolving. At age nine, what I had some control over was what I said and who I befriended. Adults could tell me who I'd live with and what to eat for dinner, but they couldn't make me talk to them or emotionally open up, so I didn't.

At school, I'd race through assigned schoolwork that my mind interpreted as someone telling me what to do so I had the freedom to read my favorite book while the rest of the class finished their assignment. Something as common as being told what's for dinner or being given an assignment by my teacher was proof to my mind that I had no freedom.

From a brain science perspective, confirmation bias was happening all over the place as my mind collected proof of my powerlessness and then fought to give me a feeling of being in control. But you can see how it was a losing battle from the start. My mind found the problem it was looking for, of course. Then it tried to give me a feeling of agency by changing things in my outside environment, but because feelings don't come from the world "out there," that was never going to work. Instead, it just reinforced my mind's position that there was a true problem.

As I got older, my mind's freedom-seeking strategies changed. Being punished as a teenager, being told I couldn't go out with my friends because I didn't follow the rules at home, for example, was that devastating moment on my purple bed all over again. So, I learned to play the game. I followed the rules (or became good at not getting caught when I didn't follow them). I got good grades and kept my room clean, not because those things mattered to me, but because they were things I could leverage in exchange for autonomy and decision-making power.

As I became an adult, my mind would talk about "covering my bases" and doing things "just in case." My actions were determined by what I thought would bring me the most choice and freedom. I got good grades in college so I'd have my choice of graduate schools, because not having a choice was the worst that could happen in my mind. I went for the highest degree and published as many papers as I could in graduate school because the more I accomplished, the less I'd be at the mercy of anyone's rules or limitations. My biggest fear was feeling trapped in a job with little freedom because I needed the income. So, I lived below my means and saved more money than I spent. A healthy financial cushion and a healthy cushion of achievements looked like security to my mind. They were insurance against being forced to do what someone else told me to do.

I realize there are many benefits to being responsible and conscientious. And the things I did are not uncommon. I'm certainly not the only person to save money and get the best education possible in order to have more choices in life. But what I want you to see is that, helpful or not, they were the strategy of an insecure, nine-year-old mind. This strategy, set in place by a scared child, ran my life for a long time.

Rather than living in the present, responsive to what occurred to me in real time, I was living from rules my mind created for me, based on my interpretation of a single moment in time, long ago.

My actions weren't coming from my true desires or real-time common sense. They were coming from a fear of being powerless, a fear of feeling what I felt in that moment when I was nine.

The precautions and accomplishments that were designed to ensure freedom *felt* imprisoning. This was my hamster wheel. Ironically, the fear of not having freedom felt so real that it took my freedom away. I chased "someday" in order to secure something that was already mine. I couldn't see that peace and security were already mine because I was too busy watching my mind trying frantically to nail them down. Living in fear of something bad happening is not what anyone wants, no matter what physical world outcomes it provides.

My nine-year-old strategies were rooted in the misunderstanding that I couldn't feel secure or happy if I didn't have power over everything in my life, but that was never going to happen. Even if my mom had agreed to never be in a relationship, something else would have come along that I had no control over. A safety net of accomplishments was never going to change that.

We are always free by virtue of our design. Our psychology will argue with the way things are, but beyond those arguments, we are secure, content, and free. A feeling of lack can only come from thought. We can feel peace at any time, within any living, work, health, or financial situation. When I was nine, I thought my mom's boyfriends could make me miserable. But that was the innocent misunderstanding of a nine-year-old.

***

Can you identify one of the strategies your mind came up with when something scary happened long ago? How does it play into your life today?

25. My Mind's Staying-Quiet Habit

The other strategy my nine-year-old brain came up with in that conversation with my mom was to keep to myself. My mind was stunned that I could be so wrong about how my opinions would be received. My mom obviously didn't care how I felt, and if my own mother didn't care, who would? I would never put myself out there like that again.

My little-kid mind reasoned that I was an inconvenience to my parents' new social lives. If they didn't care about my opinions, they didn't deserve to know me. If they wanted to know how I felt, they'd have to ask. In this way, I could exert one of the few things I did have power over. It didn't take long for staying quiet to become my new norm. Before long, it was just how I was with them and, to a lesser degree, others.

It's worth mentioning that as much as my mind convinced me that this was the best way to never feel hurt again, my nature, the nature of all people, is connection. This is clearly the case in big-picture, spiritual terms where "connection" is really a misnomer. It's not that we strive for connection, it's that we *are* connected. We are one single energy manifesting in infinite forms that look like separate you, me, him, and her, but that are only apparently separate on the surface.

Connection is our nature in evolutionary and neuroscience terms too. For the earliest humans, being socially disconnected was literally a death sentence. In terms of brain development today, we've seen too often that the human brain doesn't properly develop in isolation. We've evolved for connection with other people so much so that we experience a threat to social connection in a way that's similar to how we experience physical pain. Lack of connection literally hurts, ensuring that we stay connected and interdependent (Lieberman 2013).

This is why our ego strategies hurt—they go against our nature. While a new habit of walling off my parents and assuming no one wanted to hear what I had to say took over, my default nature moved me toward some degree of connection and sharing with them and with others. Our default nature is so strong that it finds ways of peeking through our habitual thinking, similar to how the sun peeks through the clouds. When our mind strategies are leading the charge, there will be tension. That's the tension of us moving against our nature, there to remind us that we're pushing against what's natural and true.

For someone with a "no one wants to hear you" story, it's pretty remarkable that I'm an author, teacher, and speaker today. I love how life worked this out on my behalf. My mind spent decades telling me no one wants to hear what I have to say, yet something deeper has always felt the nudge to share what I see about life more widely, and it has, despite my mind's stories. We're lived by an intelligence rooted in our natural expansiveness, *and* we live with our mind's repetitive stories and strategies. They aren't mutually exclusive—both are happening at once. Life is moving us toward the oneness that is who-we-are, and our psychology expresses itself in unique ways. There's room for both.

In many subtle and some not-so-subtle ways, these strategies shaped my life. My mind narrated life, and because I didn't realize it was a nine-year-old mind's strategies leading the charge, I listened. It told me how to be in order to make my way through life, and I followed its directions.

I realize this might sound discouraging. If all hurting, scared, little-kid minds draw strong conclusions about what's wrong and then formulate strategies to avoid those made-up wrongs, what hope do we have of *not* being led around by our mind?

We have boatloads of hope, actually.

Who-we-are is not touched by feelings of fear or insecurity or the mind strategies that are working so hard to prevent those feelings. Who-we-are is secure and thriving by nature.

Everything about our psychological experience is temporary, in motion, and relatively superficial. We feel impacted by it, no question. But the impact we feel is the moving, changing energy taking form as thoughts and feelings. It's our psychology, our human weather. Those weather patterns move through us, we feel them, and then they're promptly replaced by new human weather. It only feels personal and long-lasting because we're so tuned in to it, identifying with it as if its who-we-are. We don't see another place to look. This is why clearing up this misunderstanding naturally leaves us less identified with our experience. When we see it for what it is, it loses its grip.

In my own exploration of who-we-are and how our mind works, I've begun to wake up to what my mind says, why it says it, and importantly, who-I-am beyond those conditioned conversations.

* * *

Think of one way life lived you, aligned with your true nature, despite what your mind says.

26. My Freedom of Mind

I've come to deeply know that I am the always-free, always-well expansiveness beyond my moving, changing experience. Seeing the truth in this—not just knowing it intellectually, but having a meaningful, embodied knowing of it—means that more often than not, I am witness to the parade of experience moving through me. Insecure thoughts or feelings arise, of course. But they are passers-by. There's a growing separation between what I experience and what I call "who-I-am" or "home." There is a growing space between the thoughts and feelings that arise within me and the awareness that I know myself to be.

My mind made up some stories a long time ago. (My mind made up stories earlier today too. That's what minds do.) But I am not those stories. I navigate them more by feel than by listening to the words. I know that minds lie. They try to protect us with strategies and interpretations that are inaccurate, so listening to the content doesn't make sense. Instead, I *feel* when I'm caught up in a limiting story. The less-than-expansive feeling shows me what's going on. It shows me that I'm identified with something—a thought, concept, or false identity—that is not me or mine. It's nothing I need to hold on to or make sense of.

The feeling reminds me to let go. It reminds me who-I-am.

I feel increasingly tethered to who-I-am even when my mind is loud, bossy, and repetitive and even when my mood is low.

I've deeply seen that my habitual ways of being don't describe me much at all.

I'm not a quiet person. I'm not a guarded person or a person who loves control. I'm not a high achiever or a modest achiever or any kind of achiever. Thought that was consistent with some of those qualities moved through me in the past, and I identified with it and acted accordingly. But that no longer looks personal. We might say that was part of my personality, but even my personality doesn't look personal. It's the way energy manifested through me. A different manifestation of energy in any given moment would create different thought, different behavior, and different personality characteristics. What we call personality is, in large part, us living out our mind's old protective strategies because we don't see another option. But it was never us. Personality is like a mask we wear. You can wear the same mask for most of your life, but it's still a mask.

Now that I'm no longer so closely identified with those strategies, the frequency and urgency with which my mind tries to cover my bases, secure my freedom, and stay quiet is far less than it used to be.

These strategies are not completely gone, but it no longer feels like they need to be. I either recognize them when they arise or I notice that I feel stressed or insecure, and I know that my mind is trying to lead the charge. I remember to take myself less seriously.

Earlier today, for example, a new team member in my business produced some work that was not up to par. A rush of feelings flooded through me, smacking of "I'm powerless to get what I asked for." Objectively, the output by this new employee was not that big a deal, but it felt like one because of meaning my mind habitually attached to it.

My feelings showed me what was going on. That strong rush of energy over something I knew wasn't a tragedy reminded me that I wasn't seeing things clearly. I realized that I was seeing this through my mind's filter, and in seeing that, the thoughts and feelings dissipated very quickly. I provided some feedback and asked him to redo the task, the way I assume most people without my old mind strategy would. The old thinking came up, but it wasn't limiting or problematic.

Today, these mind strategies feel more like tendencies than directives. They feel like my mind's favorite stories, its habitual inclinations, but not things that hijack me. I have enough space and insight to notice them with detachment most of the time.

My deeper connection with who-I-am makes me increasingly sensitive to anything that doesn't feel light, open, and free. I used to live with a level of near-constant heaviness in the form of worry, low-level anxiety, and my mind's rules. From that place, I couldn't recognize my mind telling me to work harder so no one can boss me around or to be quiet because no one cared to hear from me. Those limiting thoughts felt tight, no doubt, but I rarely noticed because tight was my normal. I was the fish in water saying, "What's water?"

As I've relaxed into who-I-am, my mind is far quieter overall. So when it jumps in with a bunch of insecure thoughts and feelings, those stand in stark contrast to the peace within which they are arising. I feel them and recognize them as nothing to take too seriously. They're a mind doing what minds do.

And if I don't wake up to my experience and I take action rooted in old strategies—which absolutely happens—it's okay. Each moment is an opportunity for a do-over. Every day my mind pushes me around in ways that go unrecognized, but that's not a problem. It's part of being human.

Sometimes while I'm addressing a reader's question for my weekly *Ask Amy* video or leading a group call for The Little School of Big Change, my mind will say, "Who do you think you are? No one wants to hear what you have to say." Which is hilarious because, quite literally, someone just asked what I had to say! It's not about having freedom *from* your mind's habitual strategizing. It's about having freedom *with* a mind doing these things. What a mind does is never a problem. It's not even limiting when you see it for what it is.

These are just a couple of my mind's strategies. Everyone has their own.

Lucy's mind might have concluded that being wrong was dangerous. Her strategy was to not make waves and never make a mistake. Following her mind's strategy would keep her safe and accepted.

Hannah's mind might have concluded that her desires left her vulnerable and exposed. In her attempt to squash her desires, she ended up in a binge-and-starve cycle.

Colette's mind told her it was shameful to be seen. Everyone in her small Irish town was talking about how inferior her family was, so her mind tried to protect her by suggesting she remain unseen.

We all wear masks we put on long ago as a way to stay safe and avoid discomfort. And then we forgot we put on a mask.

But we can all remember. Exploring who-we-are and how our mind works to us allows us to finally see the mask we've been wearing. When we see that we're wearing a mask and we see how unnecessary it is, the mask loosens, and we get to see beyond it.

* * *

Imagine what it would feel like to have enough distance from your mind's habitual strategies that you feel free *with* them, if not free *of* them?

Just Another Thought

If positive thinking feels like freedom, is it okay to practice it?

Visit my website, https://www.dramy johnson.com/justathought, to hear me speak to this question.

27. Background Noise

I remember watching television with my sister when we were kids, sitting cross-legged on the carpet way too close to our small-screen color TV that sat inside a giant wooden box. Engrossed in our favorite shows, the closer we sat, the better.

Every time an adult would walk past the family room, they would tell us to back up. "It's bad for your eyes to sit that close," or "Can you even see what you're watching from up there?"

We barely heard them. The more we enjoyed the show, the closer we wanted to sit. The closer we sat, the less we noticed anything going on around us.

This was how we watched all of our favorite shows with one exception: *The Incredible Hulk*. We were obsessed with, but also terrified of Dr. Bruce Banner becoming angry, turning green, and morphing into the Hulk. We'd only watch *The Incredible Hulk* huddled together behind the couch at the far end of the room, peeking around the corner, as far away as we could to still make out what was happening on the screen. During this show, we *wanted* to hear the hum of cars driving by outside or our mom putting pots and pans away in the kitchen. Those sounds shifted our focus enough to remind us that the Hulk was only a made-up character in a television show.

Imagine a show playing on the television at your house. If you pull up a seat and sit right in front of it, your eyes and attention glued to the screen, you'll be sucked into whatever is taking place.

When you are so immersed in the show that it takes up the whole of your experience, you're pulled along for the ride. When there's a tragic scene, you're filled with sadness, a suspenseful or scary or peaceful scene, you're fully in those feelings. Your mind follows the story, and your physical body and emotions add special effects as they always do, bringing each scene to life within you. The storyline on the screen is your reality. Everything else fades away.

Now imagine that same program playing on the television, but rather than sitting up close paying attention, you're tidying up the house. You're folding laundry, sweeping floors, fluffing pillows. You can hear the show, and you're likely seeing most of it, but you're not front and center. It's more like background noise.

How emotionally pulled around are you by the scene playing out on the screen when it's background noise? Not much, right?

This is what it's like as you begin to have greater freedom of mind. Your mind is switched "on," the narrator is talking, waves of energy in the form of feelings are pulsing through you, but your face isn't pressed up against it. When your face isn't pressed up against it, it doesn't feel as consuming.

As we see more about how all minds work, we're less inclined to sit up close and hang on every word and feeling. We know it's a performance. "Based on true events" perhaps, but fictionalized and sensationalized. Our own mind is the writer, director, and producer.

We know that the scenes are constantly changing. You don't need to pause or back up the show in order to solve some problem that occurred in a previous scene. Everything you need is always here now, *beyond* the rotating storyline, characters, or props in any given scene. Who-you-are is the awareness within which every scene arises.

Our moving, changing experience is safe. It is not who-we-are, but we don't realize that as easily when we're tuned in to it in a heavy, serious way. But when we have a bit of space, we find ourselves in what Buddhists call equanimity. Experience is happening, but we are less reactive to it. It's easy to see why equanimity can feel difficult or like not the norm—our brain evolved to react to stimuli in order to keep us safe. It evolved to be very sensitive to feelings, especially feelings we experience as unpleasant, as a way to keep us vigilant and therefore alive. Reacting is just what brains do, but you can insightfully see that and rest more and more in the space around your experience. You can handle anything that moves through. It's all moving, after all, and it's all safe. This is true resilience.

People often ask: "Isn't life boring when you're onto the illusion? If my psychology becomes more like background noise and if my mind becomes still and quiet, won't that feel dull?"

A mind would ask that, wouldn't it? Actually, it's the complete opposite.

When we think our experience is all there is, ironically, we're often afraid to look at it. Believing that what we feel is objective reality is either very good news or very bad news, depending on what we feel. When it feels uncomfortable or dangerous *and* true and personal, we numb. We avoid. We look away. We distract ourselves from our experience of life in countless ways, like staying chronically busy, needing to be surrounded by people or noise, taking a victim stance and deciding "What's the point?," yielding to the myriad habits and addictions we have, and carrying on in so many other ways.

When we're spooked by our own psychology, we dance around it, sort of feeling it, sort of looking at it, but not really. We don't make eye contact with life. We're in our heads, in near-constant distraction mode because we don't feel safe in what we might feel. So, we don't take in the full experience of all that's moving through us, and *that* is what leads to a life that feels dull and flat. It's dull and flat because our mind is so busy trying to make things okay for us. Meanwhile, everything already is okay, but we're missing it.

It's never the thoughts or feelings in and of themselves that hurt or scare us. It's our misunderstanding of them. It's our relationship with our experience.

I remember realizing a level of freedom in my binge-eating habit that I never dreamed I'd have. A few months into my recovery,

I was at a place where I was no longer trying to manage my choices, urges, or thoughts. I was living life moment to moment, feeling ultimately safe in any urge or discomfort that might arise. Yet, for many months, or even years later, it wasn't uncommon for my mind to suggest a behavior around binge eating. The old, familiar "You know what would be nice right about now…" understandably still came around. My machine-mind had gone there for years—it made sense that it wouldn't completely, suddenly end.

Initially, these thoughts and feelings felt a bit dangerous. What if I listen? But over time, I began feeling waves of gratitude when these old thoughts and inclinations came up. I loved it because they showed me how much had changed. They reminded me that the only problem, ever, was fleeting experience that I saw as truth. The fact that these thoughts and urges came up, but felt so incredibly different, reminded me that I used to be sitting with my face pressed to the television.

Now, I was backed up. There was space.

* * *

Imagine feeling your mind-created experience with a bit of distance, as if it's background noise. Can you sense what a different experience that would be?

28. Paradigm Shift

The understanding of who-we-are and how all minds work that we're exploring is, in many ways, a new paradigm.

The old paradigm implies that we are our psychological experience. We are the sum of our thoughts, feelings, and behaviors. We are the "me" identity our left-brain interpreter constructs for us. We have a personality that is stable and meaningful, that tells the world who-we-are.

The new paradigm couldn't be more different. In the new paradigm, we feel psychological experience moving through us, but we know we aren't our psychology. Our psychology, which includes our mind-created identity and personality traits, is always in flux. We aren't the masks we wear.

The old paradigm says that life affects us in unfavorable ways that are felt through the whole of who-we-are. We can be irreversibly damaged by our experience.

In the new paradigm, we see that life is not about the identity we call "me." When we're caught up in experience, believing it can hurt us, we experience that. We unintentionally stare right at it when it looks like all there is. But we are incomprehensibly resilient. Our formless nature is never damaged by anything, and the form is always changing. When we see that we're undamageable, *that* becomes our reality.

In Western culture, the old paradigm says remarkably little about our formless essence, that part of us that is foundational and never changing. In the old paradigm, smart, rational, brain-led people don't concern themselves with what we can't see, touch, or measure in a laboratory.

In the new paradigm, we see that we are one formless energy taking rotating, impermanent form. When we sense a formless energy toward which to look, we feel life beyond our conditioned thinking. We look toward the pure potential, health, love, and clarity that lies within. The formless is alive. Looking toward what's already done and over, what's already taken form as a thought, feeling, or circumstance, is essentially looking at the past, toward what's dead.

The old paradigm implies that we have a lot to do. We're responsible for protecting ourselves from our passing-through experience. We're responsible for healing ourselves when we've been hurt, cheering ourselves up when we're sad, changing our thoughts, managing our anxiety, breaking our habits, and creating the change we wish to experience.

Paradigm shifts tend to be a gradual process for an individual. They are an even slower process for a society or a planet. That's one reason this book is so repetitive. Looking at the same simple ideas repeatedly, from different angles, with a variety of stories and examples, allows us to see a little more each time. Repetition begins to shift our individual paradigm slowly but surely.

The result of a paradigm shift is effortless, inevitable change.

When we see the world differently, we naturally think, feel, and behave differently. The Hindu parable of the snake and the rope is a classic illustration of this.

A man is walking alone in the desert and comes upon a rattle-snake. He panics. His body reacts in all the ways bodies react in panic—his heart is racing, he's full of adrenaline, time feels stopped, his muscles are poised to run. Before he runs, something tells him to take one final look. As he turns to glance once more at the rattlesnake, he sees that the snake is actually a rope.

The instant he sees that the snake is a rope, the fear is gone. His body chemistry immediately begins restoring to its default resting state, and the inclination to run vanishes. He couldn't make himself fear the "snake" now if he wanted to because he sees it for what it truly is.

When you deeply see that the snake is a rope, it takes no effort to not be afraid. And when you're not afraid, it takes no effort to keep hiking through the desert or whatever it is you're doing. When you deeply see that you're the most expansive oneness imaginable and the experience flowing through you is safe, impersonal, and always changing, it takes no willpower or concerted effort to change your thinking or behave differently. It's not a conscious *doing* on your part, it's an effortless *seeing*. It's a no-willpower approach.

It's not that you won't get caught up in your experience at times. You absolutely will.

It's more that overall, as your paradigm shifts, the more often you find yourself feeling who-you-are and the more things seem off when you don't feel that way. Your tolerance for feeling anything less than peace and expansiveness decreases, which is great news. Your sensitivity to discomfort works like a finely tuned instrument reminding you that you're focused on a left-brain interpretation as if it's the truth. The discomfort is there to remind you to let your mind relax so you naturally fall back into who-you-are.

The only reason it has looked like life is dangerous, we outgrow our resilience, or we are our personality is because that's what we've been led to believe. That's the paradigm we're taught implicitly and explicitly by people who were taught that paradigm themselves. We always see what we expect to see. Our efficient brain makes sure of it.

And likewise, when we know that we are actually peace, love, and wisdom with the ability to think that we aren't, we see that. Our health, resilience, peace, love, and wisdom pop out like Waldo popping out of the crowded scene. Once you've spotted him, you can't miss him.

When we open ourselves to seeing things this way, we do. And when we see differently, we do differently.

When your paradigm shifts, everything else follows.

* * *

Think of "snakes" in your own life that turned out to be "ropes." Have you found that once you see something in a new way, your feelings and behaviors naturally change too?

Just Another Thought

How can the new paradigm help with social issues and real problems on our planet?

Visit my website, https://www.dramy johnson.com/justathought, to hear me speak to this question.

29. How

A common question people ask when they begin exploring this new paradigm is "How?"

How do I stop being so caught up in everything my mind says?

How can I remember that discomfort is pointing me back home?

How do I explore the expansive peace, love, and wisdom that is my true nature?

How will my anxiety (depression, insecurity, fear, habits, etc.) eventually lift?

There's rarely a satisfactory answer to the "how" question because waking up is not something we *do*. It's the result of something we *see*. We have a paradigm shift that allows us to see life differently, and from there, we naturally, effortlessly think, feel, and act differently. There's no "how" to it.

How do you see differently? You do exactly what you're doing as you read this book. You look in a new direction with an open mind, willing to see something new. That's your only job.

When I met Linda, she was feeling helpless over her nightly wine habit. It started with an occasional glass of wine after a rough day at work. The wine felt like a magic wand that quieted her mind's rehashing and storytelling and allowed her to relax. One glass quickly turned into two or three. Two or three nights per week quickly turned into six or seven.

Linda's mind had a love-hate relationship with wine. It contradicted itself constantly. One minute, wine was the one thing that allowed her to relax and feel like herself. The next minute, it was the culprit at the center of this new problem she had. Because wine looked central to everything, it got showered with attention. Linda was always thinking about how much wine she had the night before and which actions she could take to drink less.

She wasn't aware of her habit-free, peaceful essence because she was so tuned in to her mind's conversation about how she thought, felt, and acted toward wine.

Given that wine consumption was where Linda's mind camped out, it was natural that she focused on behavior change. She read several popular psychology books about rewiring your brain to no longer want alcohol, so Linda set out to do that. Rewiring her brain was very simple, if not easy—by drinking less, she'd be teaching her brain to want alcohol less. When she stopped reinforcing the neural pathways that led to drinking, those pathways would change and soon, she wouldn't want wine at all.

Linda decided to cut down to three glasses of wine per week. She did that for a while, mostly by sheer will. When she wanted wine beyond her weekly allotment, she tried to outrun her thoughts and feelings by distracting herself from them. She spent a lot of time making plans to be with friends who didn't drink and coming up with things she could do instead when she wanted a glass of wine. It had a certain logic to it, but rearranging her life around not drinking not only became a full-time job, it kept wine on her mind more than ever. Even if she *consumed* less wine than usual, she was thinking about it more. The more she white-knuckled her way through cutting down, the more she was strengthening rather than weakening her neural pathways. That's the thing about willpower—the focus and effort it requires often has the opposite of the intended effect.

Linda knew that what she was doing wasn't working, but she didn't see another option. *Isn't this how people find freedom—by changing their behavior?* she wondered. From her current paradigm, she couldn't see another way.

One day Linda was on an online message board for people trying to stop drinking, and she saw several references to The Little School of Big Change where I help people through the new paradigm. She joined the next course and began to see her habit in a radically different way.

She began to see that her mind urged her toward wine because it equated wine with relaxation. When Linda drank, her mind often quieted. Because alcohol helped numb her busy thinking in the beginning and her mind is always looking for things that appear to be helpful, it concluded that wine is necessary for Linda's relaxation.

That conclusion became a new rule for Linda's mind. Confirmation bias led her mind to create and magnify experiences that confirmed that theory and to discount experiences that disconfirmed it (for example, all the times wine didn't lead to relaxation and the huge number of times Linda relaxed without wine).

Before long, wine looked to Linda like the fastest, easiest way to feel like who-she-is. Sometimes it felt like the *only* way for her to feel like herself, but this was only because her mind drew that conclusion and then confirmed it in her experience over and over again.

As Linda woke up to the fact that her mind was trying to help her, but that its conclusions were not accurate or helpful, she was less fooled by it. She saw the wisdom in her habit. She realized that she didn't have a hard time kicking the wine habit because she was weak or seriously addicted, it was hard because her brain mistakenly equated wine with peace. Because Linda *is* peace, there was huge momentum pulling her there.

She began to see her urges for wine more like the directives of a machine that thinks it's helping her, but that truly isn't. Her mind was like a toddler "helping" bake cookies. There ends up being more flour on the floor than in the mixer, but the child thinks they are helping. That's how our brain "helps" in the case of habits and addictions.

What if wine wasn't the magic potion Linda thought it was, that it only numbed her thinking? With her thinking numbed, she could feel who-she-is. It was her own always-there essence that she yearned to feel. Habits are not flaws or signs of weakness. They are our best attempt to find our way to the peace and expansiveness that is who-we-are. They distract us from what is in the way. The only thing ever in the way of who-we-are is psychological experience that appears real.

When Linda had some space between who-she-is and the experience moving through her, she became curious about that space. She found that in that space, she didn't want or need anything, especially not a mind-altering depressant.

Little by little, Linda began to identify with that peaceful space that wanted for nothing. It became tangible and familiar to her, and it felt like home. Her psychology didn't stop, of course. She still found her mind spinning on stressful stories about how things should have gone at work and its other favorite tales. Her mind talked about wine a fair bit too. But because she was in that more expansive, open space and because she was feeling more contentment than she had in a long time, she noticed her thoughts and feelings arising in a way she hadn't before. Emotional discomfort got her attention, not as something to frantically avoid, but as a reminder that she was caught up in her experience. It was a reminder to relax and let her experience to flow through.

Linda went from thinking that she was weak and addicted to seeing that she was neither. She was perfectly healthy. Her habit was due to a simple misunderstanding. Linda simply identified with her mind's desire for wine as if it were *her* desire.

When her mind was quiet, there was no wine story, no wine urges, no desire for anything other than what she already had. And when her mind sped up, there was a desire to feel at peace again.

She saw that, like weather clearing, her mind always settled. Her experience came and went on its own accord, without fail.

Ironically, when the focus shifted away from how much wine she drank, she found herself essentially relapse-proof. I don't mean that Linda never drank. She did turn to wine at times, when she was feeling especially low. But without a story that she was weak or would always have this problem, it looked like feedback, not a problem. If anything, these episodes helped her see things more clearly.

As Linda felt more connected with her peaceful home base and her experience looked safer and less personal, the benefits of drinking rapidly dwindled. Even if her machine-mind habitually brought it up, the suggestion had no sticking power because there was much less discomfort for drinking to numb. With nothing to numb, wine lost its appeal.

This is how seeing life in a new way deeply changes things. Our behavior changes, but we don't start there. Jumping into behavior change before we've seen things differently requires discipline and often feels like white-knuckling. But when we have a paradigm shift, our habits no longer feel desirable because what they're designed to numb—our experience—no longer needs to be numbed.

Linda's habit naturally tapered off. It wasn't particularly difficult. It felt uncomfortable at times, but feeling discomfort wasn't as horrible as it used to be. She knew her feelings were energy with a habitual "this hurts" story. Seeing feelings this way allowed the story to play as background noise and eventually fall away. Even when Linda's experience didn't feel like background noise, when she was very much caught up in it, she deeply knew that it was experience. Anything that hurts is.

The change she experienced was as foundational as it gets. It wasn't about drinking per se, and there was nothing to apply. Her problem was not about alcohol dependence. It was an innocent case of mistaken identity. There was nothing to do, nothing to cope with, and nothing to manage.

When she was using willpower to change her behavior, her change strategy required her to be hypervigilant to any thought or feeling that felt like an urge to drink. She had to be on the lookout so she could jump in and distract herself from anything she didn't want to feel.

When Linda woke up to who-she-is and saw her experience for what it is, the hypervigilance was replaced with space and equanimity. With nothing to manage and nothing to fear, her mind thought about drinking far less and eventually, not at all. This is how neural pathways are changed and brains "rewire" when we relax. We see the truth, and our attention naturally shifts. We don't have to remove our attention from our psychological experience. It shifts from our fleeting psychology to our stable essence on its own.

If seeing things in a new way leads to sustainable, relatively graceful change, why do we so often try to change our behavior first?

In part, because your mind will convince you that it's in charge. Your safety is your mind's number one job—it's no wonder it wants to take charge of breaking your habits and creating paradigm shifts for you.

And with your mind leading the way, of course it will focus on behavior. Behavior is the visible, tip of the iceberg that minds see. Manipulating your visible behavior looks to your mind like the direct route.

We live in a society rooted in the old paradigm, which views our moving, changing psychological experience as something we need to manage and control. We aren't told that our experience moves through on its own. Instead, the predominant conversation is about which levers we can pull in order to make things different, preferably as quickly as possible. To a mind that loves control, a five-step strategy, hack, or miracle technique is a dream come true.

Most self-help books are full of behavioral steps, but I would argue that those behaviors aren't what led to the author's change—insight did. A paradigm shift allowed people to naturally behave differently, and then those people—in their innocent desire to help others—share the behavioral steps because that's what we're used to writing about. That's the paradigm most of the world lives in.

Take, for example, popular advice about waking up early and doing the most important things, especially creative ventures, before anything else. This will be helpful advice for some people, and I'm sure it's been helpful for the people touting it. But it's also going to be horrible advice for others, right? It would be horrible advice for me. I'm at my best early in the morning, but I know myself, and there's no way I could wake up and throw myself into creative ventures. I like to exercise and take care of more immediate tasks first, which feels like it frees my mind to ease into more thoughtful projects a bit later.

Someone stumbles upon something that works for them or they have an insight that has them seeing life differently, and they do what is natural to them from the way life looks. Then, rooted in the old paradigm, they focus on behavior to the exclusion of everything else. They share the behaviors as if that's what matters most, but it's actually what matters least.

This goes for almost all advice, including how to eat, handle relationship issues, and parent your children. The advice-giver is sharing what works for them from their current paradigm. They say, "Do these things, and you'll have the experience I had," but it doesn't work that way. Most advice is someone else's insights revealed to them, repackaged and presented by them as a series of behavioral steps. But those to-do's were only easy and effective for the advice giver because of the initial insights they had.

Insight is sustainable. Paradigm shifts are sustainable. Advice, how-to steps, willpower, and effort are surface-level, shallow, and relatively temporary.

When I help people find freedom from habits and anxiety in The Little School of Big Change, I often want to use the term "fall away" to describe how their issues change. When we see things for what they are, habits and anxiety serve no purpose, and they eventually fall away.

To be honest, I cringe a little when I say this, especially to people who are new to this paradigm. It sounds too good to be true, doesn't it? It sounds like something you'd hear on an infomercial. "Buy now, and your issues will magically fall away! And wait, there's more! Other things in your life that you didn't realize were problems will fall away too!"

But it's not magic. It's how we wake up to the healthy, peaceful essence, always there beyond our psychological experience. It's how everything changes, from the way we see life, to our neural circuitry, to our relationship with our thoughts, feelings, and behaviors.

Notice that only a computer-mind, always looking for a job, asks, *How?* It operates in directions, steps, and action. Who-you-are gets that life doesn't work that way. Who-you-are knows that seeing clearly does all of the work.

So when you find yourself asking *How?* see that as feedback that your mind is active. It's trying to manage your change, but minds are horrible at managing change. Change doesn't need to be managed. It happens naturally as you see differently.

* * *

Can you think of things that have "fallen away" in your life when your understanding of them changed?

30. There Is Nothing in Your Future

Say this aloud: "I don't know."

It feels good, doesn't it?

There is enormous freedom in remembering how little we actually know.

Our mind talks nonstop about everything it thinks it knows. It fills in the blanks of what it doesn't know to sound like it does know. It's a big ole' know-it-all.

It does this because it loves us, because it equates knowing with our security and survival. But as we've seen throughout this book, our mind's reasons and conclusions are often inaccurate. Our mind's theories, often formed in moments of insecurity, consist of made-up rules about how we need to be in order to survive.

It's said that the human brain processes eleven million bits of information per second, but we are consciously aware of only about fifty bits per second. Isn't that an incredible ratio? Eleven million bits of information, give or take, are being taken in and processed every single second, but only fifty out of those eleven million are known to us. The overwhelming majority of what is taken in, is filtered out.

How do you suppose our brain decides what to bring to life in consciousness and what to filter out and ignore? Since our brain is all about certainty and efficiency, it brings to life what is familiar and known. It favors information that supports its theories. Surprises are too risky, and inconsistencies require too much energy to resolve.

In the name of certainty, our mind creates assumptions and expectations about the future. It tells us how life goes for "people like us." It paints pictures of what life will look like "someday," and we live in the narrow range of those stories whether we realize it or not.

To see if your mind is doing this, ask yourself, "What's likely in my future?"

I bet your mind has an answer for you.

Does the future feel limitless and full of pure possibility? If not, your mind is projecting a limited idea of "you" in some other space and time, passing it off as "what's likely to happen for someone like me."

Anything a mind creates about you or your future—whether it's small and dreadful or vast and exciting—is incredibly limited relative to the actual realm of possibility. It has to be because a mind made it up. As machines, minds play in what they know. What your mind brings to the task of predicting the future is what it has already seen. Do you know another name for what your mind has already seen? The past.

When your mind—in real time—creates thoughts, expectations, and images that it says are about "the future," it's using known information. It's like if you were to write a book using only the documents already stored on the hard drive of your computer.

You could do it. You might even be able to write a pretty creative book by rearranging and editing what's already been created. But it's not going to be as fresh or inspired as if you were to set all of that aside and let something brand new flow through you in real time.

The concept of "the future" that our mind cooks up is like that book written from the documents you already have saved. It's a slightly rearranged, slightly revised, perhaps slightly improved version of the past.

Maybe you show up as a slightly improved version of who you think you are now. You have some different qualities, your life has changed in some ways, but it's a matter of degree rather than a matter of actual change. You may see yourself in the future having moved up in your company, with improved health and maybe more confidence or clarity. But do you see how the picture is still rooted in what's already been created? Your mind takes a snapshot of "you" or "your life" or "who you are" as it sees you, adds a little here or a little there, and then calls that your future.

Or maybe it takes a snapshot of your life today and takes a bit away. If you feel a sense of doom or foreboding for the future, your mind is doing this. You're still you, but you're worse for the wear in all the predictable places.

It will only show up in the predictable places. If your financial status is a big part of your life today, your assumed future includes it. If that's not something you think about much, it might not. Just like your brain shows you only fifty of the eleven billion bits of information it takes in, your mind-created future revolves around the relatively tiny subset of images and topics that already happen to be on your mind. It's all quite predictable because it's a mind playing in what it thinks it already knows.

It's a made-up picture, placed in a made-up time, passed off as real.

Because it's passed off as real, and it has been for as long as we can remember, we live as if it's real. Our mind's calculation of the future limits us today. "People like me" don't experience that much change, we say as we see transformation happening for others. "People like me" don't get cancer, or get divorced, or experience deep, lasting peace of mind, or financial security, or move out of the country. In my case, "people like me" don't get what they want. The future your mind assumes for you is based around a largely invisible "people like me" story that plays even when we aren't aware of it.

The opposite of a "people like me" story is "I don't know."

The opposite of a made-up picture, placed in a made-up time, passed off as real is looking toward formless energy, watching it take shape through you in real time, unbound by how it took shape before. It may be shaped and influenced by what you've already done and seen, or it may not be. Who knows?

The future is empty, wide open, full of the same creative potential that creates planets and changes seasons. When there are no "people like me," anything is possible. When there is no past-based starting point, anything is possible. Any thought or feeling can arise within you. Any physical circumstance can come to pass.

The past can't create. It's done and over. Its creative power is zapped. Formless energy—not yet turned to form—is the only thing that can create, so it makes sense to look there, doesn't it? It's like looking at the source of a waterfall versus looking at the pool of water at the foot of the waterfall. Which feels more alive?

The only way our mind knows how to create is by looking to what it already knows, what's been done already, and formulating guesses based on that. It doesn't know to look toward formless energy. It isn't capable of seeing around itself. But *you* are. Who-you-are can see around what's already formed and toward the formless source of everything.

It may seem like your mind makes accurate predictions at times, but consider that what's happening is that our expectations about what happens for "people like us" creates our experience. Remember Colette, who had a habitual inclination to hide from people in social situations? When her mind says, "Everyone is judging you," she can't help but see people staring at her. She can't help but hear judgment in her neighbors' voices. Not because she's accurately predicting their judgment, but because she sees everything through a veil of habitual thought that creates her reality. It's like wearing yellow-tinted glasses and understandably, claiming that reality is yellow.

When we sense who-we-are beyond our thinking, we feel our way into a completely empty moment, pregnant with the possibility of anything but full of nothing. The left-brain-created identity "you" isn't there. Your identity is created and recreated in each and every moment. There is no slightly better or slightly worse version of "you" camped out, waiting for you.

Your stuff isn't there. Your partner, as you see him or her in this instant, isn't there.

Nothing is there, and that means absolutely anything can show up there.

Your brain will pull its concepts of you and your life through time to some extent, of course. It's what minds do. But when you feel that happening, you don't have to live within the confines of it.

The feeling of limitation or familiarity will wake you up to it. When you feel like only a sliver of the expansiveness of the entire universe is available to you, that feeling will wake you up and you'll know that your mind is running the show. You'll remember to stop and take a wider view, beyond what your mind thinks it knows.

We get to discover what wants to happen. Not what our mind tells us should happen. What wants to happen through us.

The future is utterly and completely empty.

* * *

How does it feel to consider that there is absolutely nothing in your future?

31. Perspective

I have a framed picture of Planet Earth, taken from outer space, hanging on my office wall. I love looking at that picture, especially when my mind is caught up in something that feels personal and up to me to figure out.

When we press our noses to the television screen, we're oblivious to everything around us, and we lose ourselves in that narrow reality. When we hop in a spaceship and look down on life from outer space, reality expands exponentially. Nothing has changed, but everything is different.

From up in our spaceship, "me" and "my problems" disappear. Concepts like good and bad, and right and wrong disappear. Categories like black, white, and brown, man and woman, us and them disappear. Labels like depressed, stuck, confused, and anxious disappear.

From up in our spaceship, we see that everything is in motion. The entire planet is spinning in motion. The earth itself is always contracting and expanding, dehydrating and rehydrating, moving toward death and then coming back to life. Everything on the earth—the oceans, the weather, the plant and animal life—is in constant motion.

We are part of that always in-flux flow of nature. The people on earth, who don't look separate from outer space, are going through the same things the planet is going through. Physical bodies are being born, aging, and dying. Our mental and emotional experience is swirling through us like the weather swirls in the atmosphere. Thought rises and falls within us, feelings contract and expand through us, identities are gripped and then released, problems occur and then fall away.

We see that everything is always changing from outer space. But down on earth in our tiny corner of the planet, with the tiny subset of people we know, seeing through the fifty tiny, biased bits of information that our me-centered brain shows us each second, we don't see that life is always changing. Things look static and serious. Down on earth, my world revolves around me, and yours revolves around you. We hear the narrator as if it speaks the truth. Down on earth, our happiness, peace of mind, and survival look fragile and like our responsibility.

One of the most amazing things about being human is that we get to experience life from both extremes and from every point in between. We're constantly sliding along the continuum, shifting perspectives, experiencing different realities.

We get to play down on earth, in the me-centric, separate-self, physical-world, psychological, black-and-white, cause-and-effect, close-up view of life. This perspective has everything a full-contact, realistic game should. It has you as the main character, along with a large cast of supporting characters. It has obstacles, choices, preferences, opinions, dreams, wishes, and worries, all of which serve to define the hero or heroine and his or her separation from everyone else. It has seemingly high stakes—the ability to win or lose at this game of life. It has an incredible level of detail and variety, where any psychological experience is possible.

And then, even while still planted firmly on earth, we get to transcend the game of life and see things from the outer space perspective where we are one, formless energy taking temporary, revolving form. As we blast off into space, we travel away from labels and buckets and categories to see that there's just life, energy, God, oneness.

We tend to be far more acquainted with the close-up view, don't we? Our mind is loud and familiar, and the world around us is full of shiny objects that grab our attention. But just as our immersion in our physical reality makes it sometimes difficult for us to sense the expansive oneness in all things, having glimpsed the oneness makes it harder to be fully immersed in separation. It's like a film director watching the film she helped create. She can enjoy the finished product, but she isn't as fooled by the suspenseful plot twist when she remembers yelling "Cut!" umpteen times to reapply the actors' fake blood during filming. She has insider knowledge that allows her to enjoy the illusion, but not be hoodwinked by it. So do you. The more we've glimpsed who-we-are, the less we find ourselves completely fooled—for long periods of time, anyway—by our mind's stories about the game of life. When you've seen that the snake is a rope, you can't make yourself afraid.

When I train Change Coaches to work from the new paradigm, we talk about these perspective shifts as zooming in and zooming out. On an individual level, especially when we're suffering, we're zoomed in. We're as collapsed as we can be with the stories flowing through us, temporarily forgetting the truth of who-we-are. As we relax, we naturally zoom out.

Down on earth, there are a million stories and problems, and we're swimming in all the details. But from up in space, I imagine looking down at little specks of light on earth—all of these wise, perfect little bundles of energy we call people—each with a thought cloud like you see in comic books above their head.

When you're too far away to make out the contents of their thought clouds, you see things very simply: they are caught up in thought or they aren't. They are zoomed in on their mind's stories, living from that reality, or they have relatively little in their thought cloud, which leaves them zoomed out, living in a more expansive reality.

We zoom in and out on a macro level as well. The old paradigm in mental health is zoomed in. It focuses on our separateness as individuals. It often looks at our mind's stories in an analytical way, analyzing *what* we think and feel rather than seeing *that* we think and feel. It offers a slew of techniques and strategies designed to fix, change, and manipulate how we feel. It revisits the past and, in some cases, involves hours upon hours of analyzing the content of our me-centered thinking.

At the far zoomed-out extreme might be a philosopher or spiritual teacher who only speaks to the spiritual nature of life with little regard for a person's psychological experience. Camping out in either extreme has limitations because the entire spectrum is part of our experience of being alive. Neither side is better than the other. Ease in life comes from seeing that we're naturally sliding between these two extremes all the time. Our reality is constantly shifting. We get to have an experience of ourselves as separate, and we also get to fall into our true oneness. Our feelings show us where we are along the spectrum. When we feel discomfort, we know that we're zoomed in, and we can simply let our mind relax and watch ourselves zoom out.

This conversation about perspective reminds me of the ancient Buddhist teaching by Qingyuan Weixin that's often shortened to "Mountain, no mountain, mountain."

Qingyuan Weixin says, "Before I had studied Chan (Zen) for thirty years, I saw mountains as mountains, and rivers as rivers. When I arrived at a more intimate knowledge, I came to the point where I saw that mountains are not mountains, and rivers are not rivers. But now that I have got its very substance, I am at rest. For it's just that I see mountains once again as mountains, and rivers once again as rivers."

At first, we see mountains as mountains and rivers as rivers. We see things as they appear to be, as our psychology presents them to us, as we've been taught and conditioned to see them. A mountain is a mountain with the physical traits, labels, and characteristics we've been taught to associate with a mountain.

It's the same with who-we-are. We see ourselves as Amy, Lucy, Hannah, Colette, Bethany, Matthew, and Ben. We see our identities, full of past and future behaviors, traits and characteristics, habits and mental stories, as rock solid. We see our experience—fleeting thoughts and feelings—as unmoving as mountains.

Then, we zoom out and see that mountains are not mountains and rivers are not rivers. We see that everything is made of one formless essence taking temporary form. Mountains, rivers, you, me, and all of our physical and psychological experience are temporary manifestations of one infinite, life energy. Our mind slaps labels on everything we perceive as separate and distinct, but labels are simply labels. Words and labels aren't what they represent.

Again, it's the same with who-we-are. Energy moves through us taking shape as thoughts and feelings, but we aren't those thoughts and feelings or their labels and names. We don't feel anxiety or depression or fear or insecurity. We feel fluctuations of energy with a label-laden story attached. Mountains are not mountains, and rivers are not rivers. We see our true nature and the true nature of life. We see that we're not truly separate, although we appear so. We are processes, not objects.

And now, as we end this book, we come full circle. Mountains are mountains, and rivers are rivers. Because we've seen a far bigger picture of who-we-are, we have a different zoomed-in experience.

We get to think and feel, and watch our mind worry, compare, problem solve, dramatize, and so many things a mind does, and we get to have a new experience of it.

We get to see it as just a little more like background noise and a little bit less like all-there-is.

We get to see that our mind does what it does because it loves us, but that we already, always have everything we could ever want or need.

You get to travel the continuum, zooming in and zooming out, being fully in the experience of mountains and no mountains, having experiences of who you think you are and who-you-truly-are.

Nothing is all that serious and scary when we see that everything is always changing. Every thought, every feeling, every fluctuation of energy is safe and in motion.

Well, everything except who-you-are. That's the one thing that never changes.

* * *

Notice throughout your day how zoomed in versus zoomed out you are. Your feelings will show you.

CONCLUSION

There was a student in one of my The Little School of Big Change classes last year who, about halfway through the course, said, "I don't want to look in the direction of habits and anxiety anymore. It no longer makes sense to look at what's always changing. I want to look in the direction of what is real and never changing."

We actually had been looking toward who-we-are since day one of the course, but her mind was still habitually staring at her experience. She heard me pointing toward who-she-is, but she didn't *hear* me.

Until that moment.

Her comment showed that her tolerance for identifying with her moving, changing experience had lowered. She wasn't as interested in the form anymore. She was hungry for more of the formless.

I hope that in seeing "that's just what minds do," you find yourself less caught up when your mind does those things. I hope that your mind's categorizing and worrying, labeling, and dot-connecting don't look personal or meaningful in the way they may have before. I hope that they look more like a machine doing what that machine does.

We aren't looking at what all minds do for the sake of hanging out in thought and feeling—we're looking at what all minds do so we understand it. And we're trying to understand it so we can see beyond it. When we aren't caught up in our experience, there's space to feel what else is there.

You're seeking to provide space around your human experience so you can feel your way home. Feeling into your formless essence takes care of all problems, all habits, all negative thought. It's the most practical, simple, profound thing a human can do.

You've been seeing who and what you aren't so you can discover more of who and what you are. And this is just the beginning. It's like stepping outside and realizing there's a whole new world out there that you've never seen because you thought your house was all there was. You now know this other world exists. Next, you get to explore it. There is no end to what we can discover about who-we-are. And in my experience, the more we explore, the better it gets.

ACKNOWLEDGMENTS

I'd like to thank Naphtali Visser, Phil Hughes, Tamar DeJong, and Jules Swales for helpful comments on an early draft of this book, and Naf, Phil, and the LSBC Community for copious discussions about the title.

Thank you to my agent, Steve Harris, and to everyone at New Harbinger who worked hard to make this book the best it could be.

I'm so grateful for The Little School of Big Change community and my Change Coaches for your openness and willingness to explore with me. Most of what I've seen has come from real-time discussions with you. I'm super grateful to Amanda Jones for being such an integral part of LSBC, and to Amanda, Jessica Silverman, and Jessica Smith for supporting our community with love and wisdom.

Thank you to Giles Croft for *The Secret Life of Waves*.

Thank you to my business team, Dror Amir, Nipper Sorensen, Jonathan Avigdori, and Michael Cuenco, for helping me share this understanding as far and wide as possible.

I have enormous gratitude for more teachers and colleagues than I could possibly list. Special thanks to Barb Patterson, Scott Kelly, Angus Ross, and Rohini Ross for seeing more for me than I can see myself.

Most of all, my family. Willow and Miller, you're the reason I want the world to see who-we-are. And Ora, you're the best partner—in every possible way—I could ever ask for.

ADDITIONAL
RESOURCES

To access the free resources mentioned throughout this book, please visit https://www.dramyjohnson.com/justathought.

The Little School of Big Change
If you'd like to explore who-you-are and what minds do, with my guidance and along with an incredible community, check out The Little School of Big Change: https://www.thelittleschoolofbig change.com.

Change Coach Training
If you'd like to help others find freedom of mind, please check out my Change Coach Certification Program at https://dramyhohn son.com/change-coach-training-certification/.

References

Alberini, C. M. 2010. "Long-Term Memories: The Good, the Bad, and the Ugly." *Cerebrum* (September–October): 21.

Barrett, L. F. 2020. *Seven and a Half Lessons About the Brain.* New York: Houghton Mifflin Harcourt.

Cacioppo, J. T., S. Cacioppo, and J. K. Gollan. 2014. "The Negativity Bias: Conceptualization, Quantification, and Individual Differences." *Behavioral and Brain Sciences* 37, no. 3: 309–310.

Edelman, G. 1990. *The Remembered Present: A Biological Theory of Consciousness.* New York: Basic Books.

Gazzaniga, M. S. 1985. *The Social Brain: Discovering the Networks of the Mind.* New York: Basic Books.

Korzybski, A. 1933. *Science and Sanity: An Introduction to Non-Aristotelian Systems and General Semantics.* Institute of General Semantics, 747–761.

Leary, M., and C. Cottrell. 1999. "Evolution of the Self, the Need to Belong, and Life in a Delayed-Return Environment." *Psychological Inquiry* 10: 229–232.

Lieberman, M. D. 2013. *Social: Why Our Brains Are Wired to Connect.* New York: Crown.

Malone, D., dir. 2011. *The Secret Life of Waves.* BBC.

Martin, L. 1999. "ID Compensation Theory: Some Implications of Trying to Satisfy Immediate-Return Needs in a Delayed-Return Culture." *Psychological Inquiry* 10: 195–208.

Nickerson, R. S. 1998. "Confirmation Bias: A Ubiquitous Phenomenon in Many Guises." *Review of General Psychology* 2, no. 2: 175–220.

Niebauer, C. 2019. *No Self, No Problem: How Neuropsychology Is Catching Up to Buddhism.* San Antonio: Hierophant.

Nisbett, R. E., and T. D. Wilson. 1977. "Telling More Than We Can Know: Verbal Reports on Mental Processes." *Psychological Review* 84: 231–259.

Panksepp, J. 1998. *Affective Neuroscience: The Foundations of Human and Animal Emotions.* New York: Oxford University Press.

Ross, L. 1977. "The Intuitive Psychologist and His Shortcomings: Distortions in the Attribution Process." In *Advances in Experimental Social Psychology,* edited by L. Berkowitz. New York: Academic Press, 173–220.

Taylor, J. B. 2006. *My Stroke of Insight: A Brain Scientist's Personal Journey.* New York: Penguin.

Wilson, T. D., and D. T. Gilbert. 2003. "Affective Forecasting." *Advances in Experimental Social Psychology* 35: 345–411.

Amy Johnson, PhD, is a coach, author, and speaker who shares a new paradigm for how our mind works that leads to lasting freedom from anxiety, depression, insecurity, and unwanted habits. She is author of *Being Human* and *The Little Book of Big Change*, and has been a regularly featured expert on *The Steve Harvey Show* and in *The Wall Street Journal*.

MORE BOOKS from
NEW HARBINGER PUBLICATIONS